STARS YOU NEVER SAW BEFORE

Leonard W. Mann

STARS YOU NEVER SAW BEFORE

ISBN 0-89536-159-0

PRINTED IN U.S.A.

CONTENTS

CONTENTS

A Word Concerning What Follows

Writing of the incomparable Christ, of his mission to humankind, and of what he does, Alfred Tennyson gave us these memorable lines:

He wakes desires you never may forget:
He shows you stars you never saw before:
He makes you share with him forevermore
The burden of the world's divine regret.

Stars you never saw before! They are there all right — out beyond the ordinary routines of the commonplace, beyond the daily necessities of our living and the mundane requirements which impose themselves upon us.

And we need to see those stars. Many of us, burdened with the varied demands which press in upon us, are like the harried homemaker, chafed by many chores and the multiplicity of pesky little routines, who sighed and said, "Living is so daily." It is with real insight that someone has written, "If you have two loaves of bread, sell one and buy a hyacinth."

Life's daily-ness is evident in hours of labor, deadlines to be met, burdens to be borne. But life's eternal-ness is also real, and we can see it mirrored in the heavens if only we can see the stars. Life's daily-ness is redeemed by its eternal-ness; a common drudgery is lifted by an eternal meaning. Emerson was giving some very good advice in his famous line, "Hitch your wagon to a star." The wagon is an altogether earthly vehicle, but only hitch it up to a star, and it becomes a chariot of excitement. Out of the sorrow and pain of World War I, the soldier-poet Joyce Kilmer put it this way:

Because the way was steep and long,
And through a strange and lonely land,
God placed upon my lips a song,
And put a lantern in my hand.

Christ came on a mission to our human hearts. Tennyson was right: "He wakes desires you never may forget: He shows you stars you never saw before." He is awakening us and pointing us to something beyond. This he has come to do, and this he is doing; and how desperately we need to have it done. Jesus often said, "He who has ears to hear, let him hear." I think he is also saying, "He who has eyes to see, let him see."

Remember *Pilgrim's Progress*, that remarkable allegory by John Bunyan? Christian and Hopeful had long been in the dark valley. Then shepherds took them to the mountain top. From there, through the "perspective glass," they viewed the Heavenly City. How deeply do our hearts hunger for some shepherd to guide us to the mountain, to place the "perspective glass" in our hands, and to help us see. In a modern drama one asks another, "Have you reached the heights?" And the other replies, "No, but I saw them once, and they are there all right." That glimpse can make all the difference in the world.

The Christ who came into our world long ago comes from a star-lighted manger, by way of his own dark valley, to stand beside us, here, now, and to point the way up and beyond and on. He would push back the curtains that shroud our lives, the narrow horizons that fence us in. He would awaken desires we never knew were sleeping within us, and show us stars we never saw before.

Sometimes during Advent and at Christmas time we read a remarkable thing from Isaiah chapter forty. Sometimes we sing it, for much of this is incorporated in Handel's mighty masterwork, *The Messiah*. In the familiar language of the King James version of our Scripture, here it is:

The voice of him that crieth in the wilderness,
Prepare ye the way of the Lord, make straight
in the desert a highway for our God. Every
valley shall be exalted, and every mountain

*and hill shall be made low; and the crooked shall
be made straight, and the rough places plain:
And the glory of the Lord shall be revealed, and
all flesh shall see it together: for the mouth of
the Lord hath spoken it.* [*Isaiah 40:3-5*]

Yes, perhaps this is merely a reassuring word from
the prophet to the people concerning their successful
return to Palestine from the Babylonian captivity;
perhaps it is saying that their way will be made easy.
But it is also certainly saying something else.
Attempting the journey from Babylon to Jerusalem,
those ancient Jews were not the last people to try to
go somewhere. Our living is also a kind of journey —
and there are valleys and mountains and rough places.
And if this word is to us — and I think it is — it is
saying that our valleys shall be exalted and our rough
places shall be made plain; for as we make our journey
home, the great Highway Engineer is with us
preparing the road that will take us there. The
exaltation of the valley! Whatever the valley is, Christ
is exalting it, lifting it up. And he wants us to know
that he is. He wants the pilgrim up to where he can
see the stars.

In the remarkable poem "God's Funeral," the poet
Thomas Hardy portrays himself as the spectator who
views the mournful entourage slowly moving across
the dismal and darkened plain. The foremost bear the
mystic form of the God they believe is dead, and all
are "lined on the brows, scoop-eyed and bent and
hoar." Downcast and devoid of hope, the procession
moves in silence through the dark. But there are "a
certain few who stand aloof" and say,

*See you upon the horizon that small light —
Swelling somewhat?*

but each mourner shakes his head; none can believe
the light is there; and the procession moves
dispiritedly on. And the poet concludes:

*Thus dazed and puzzled 'twixt the gleam and
gloom,*

Mechanically I followed with the rest.

Yes, there is a lot of gloom in the world. But there is also the gleam. And each of us lives somewhere between that gloom and that gleam. Some, apparently overwhelmed by the gloom, are tragically unable to see the gleam at all. May we have the eyes to see it, and to see that indeed it is "swelling somewhat." This, I believe, is of urgent importance to us as we make our journey across this landscape of years that we call life.

The Gospel According to John begins by telling the Advent-Christmas story from a perspective significantly different from Matthew or Luke. Matthew tells of wise men and a star. Luke tells of shepherds and an angelic song. But John tells of neither. Here the writer simply says that the "Word was made flesh and dwelt among us," (1:14 K.J.) and that in him was life, and the life was the light of men" (1:4 K.J.). And what does the light do? John says it shines into the darkness (1:5). This is John's dramatic portrayal of the coming of Christ: he is heaven's life-giving light shining into our darkness.

"And the darkness has not overcome it" (1:5 RSV). Not that the darkness hasn't tried. It has. But it has failed. Here is one thing that all the darkness of this world cannot do: it cannot put out this light — cannot overthrow it, destroy it, demolish it, dissolve it, or bring it to naught. At least it hasn't yet; and our faith is that it never will. The failure of the darkness! The unextinguishable light! He who has come is present. And his presence makes a dynamic difference. Not just a difference out there in our world, but a difference in us — mostly in us, you and me. At least he can make a difference, and, thank God, he often does. Tennyson's line is an appropriate one: "He shows you stars you never saw before."

That the coming and presence of Christ makes a very real and practical difference — this is the thesis and theme of these next pages. Following the Lectionary Readings for Advent and Christmas and the time immediately thereafter, these eight messages are really one message, a message of brightness, encouragement, and hope, designed to put a halo of glory around the common routines of our daily living.

As you read, I ask that you use your imagination. As I have written, I have used mine. I was invited to write a series of sermons; and what follows is just that, a series of sermons. I have imagined myself in a pulpit standing in the presence of a typical congregation; I have imagined myself preaching. As I have written, I have not visualized someone sitting somewhere reading; rather I have seen before me an audience of my fellow-pilgrims on the journey of life, with you among them. The message is addressed. I have written as I would preach — to you.

While I have often quoted from the Bible, this is not a series of Bible studies. It is intended to be inspirational preaching. In citing biblical references I have not, therefore, gone into a critical examination of context or made an analysis of possible alternate meanings or interpretations. The quotations are not limited to a single translation, and in some instances quotations appear in a composite of two or more translations. The Revised Standard Version is used most, but various others are also included. To avoid interruption of the flow of thought, I have not digressed to discuss translations or to identify them.

As you receive the message of these pages, it will be most meaningful to you if you can "hear" these words as being *said*, rather than merely see them as something to read. To experience this bonus dimension of value, if circumstances permit, be your own "preacher" and read aloud, with expression. But however you go about it, my prayer is that you may experience the Living Presence and that he may show to you — for all conditions of your life — some stars that you've never seen before.

Leonard W. Mann

The Art of Living Until

Matthew 24:37-44
"If the householder had known . . ."

There are many things about your life which I do
not know. But one thing I do know: you are living in
an interim. And so am I. We are in time-in-between;
we are between what has happened and what will
happen. We know a great deal about the former and
very little about the latter. What has been is past, and
we are moving away from it, going on to what is to be
How we make this journey is very important, the
attitudes with which we travel, the guiding stars we
follow. So I want to speak with you about *The Art of
Living Until*. This is what we are all doing — we are
living until, until . . . something.

On one occasion Jesus was telling his disciples
about some spectacular events which were yet to
come, and they asked him, "When shall these things
be?" (Matthew 24:3). In his response Jesus told them
that there would be wars and rumors and deceit,
"but," said he, "the end is not yet" (Matthew 24:6).
The end is not yet! Underline that. Accent it.
Emphasize it any way you can; because it is the basic
truth of our existence and of our living.

We all live under the canopy of one over-arching
fact: we are on our way somewhere. This is an
impression we cannot escape. The awareness comes up
from deep within us; things will not always be as they
are now. Out of all that is past, we have come to right
now. And now we are moving from what is to what
will be, going on from here to somewhere out yonder.
This is a universal truth for our humankind. Whatever
our personal circumstances or age, this truth is one we
cannot escape.

Here arise all our hopes and all our fears. For all

our hopes are for the future, and all our fears are of it. Here are rooted both our dreads and our anticipations.

The very small child forsees the time when he can ride a bike, toss a ball, move into the world of big boys and girls. And how quickly he comes to that time! The older child dreams of the teen-age years, of getting a license to drive a car, of privilege and excitement. And how quickly the years pass and the time comes! The teen-age youth anticipates the world of adult life, wanting to be his own boss, to be in command. And ah! so soon he arrives in that world. The adult man lives out his years in the daily consciousness of change, and the passing days will not let him forget duties and deadlines and prospects that loom out there ahead of him. And the older we get the more sure we are that the interim between *what is* and *what's next* is getting shorter and shorter.

Things are moving — toward something. And we are swept along with the tide. We know that, wherever we are, we are somewhere this side of something out yonder. This engenders a kind of "interim psychology," a syndrome of the temporary. And this can be dangerous. The result for most of us most of the time is a kind of *carpe diem* complex. We want to sieze the day, the present day, to grasp it, to grab it. But what for? with what in view? to what purpose? to what end?

I suppose there are, in general, two ways to use the day. One is mentioned in Isaiah 22:13 where a group of people are described as slaying oxen and killing sheep and eating flesh and drinking wine and saying, "Let us eat and drink, for tommorow we die." Well, this is one approach to interim living, a very tragic and prodigal approach. It is living as though the interim is all there is.

This way is to squeeze life for its very last dregs, to wrest from it the last small smidgins of pleasure before, presumably, it's too late; and this way has some aspects of panic. Not long ago a popular song advised, "Kiss her now." Kiss her right now — while she's yours; while you've got the chance, grab the opportunity. On a young man's powerful sports car I saw a bumper sticker bearing this message: "If it feels good, do it." This is saying there is only one consideration — how it feels, now. No matter what doing it does, do it. Whatever shackles it puts upon the future, go ahead — today is all that matters. And even it matters only because it offers a chance to grab something from it.

Back in the seventeenth century British poet Robert Herrick wrote a thing he entitled "To the Virgins" in which he advised, "Gather ye rosebuds while ye may," saying don't miss your chance, for the time will come when you may not. And, my dear friend, on any day during which we encounter any substantial number of other persons, we are very likely to see several whose philosophy of interim living is simply and tragically this: Let us eat and drink, for tomorrow we die, or, tomorow something else may happen.

But there is another philosophy. And Jesus speaks of it in the twenty-fourth chapter of Matthew, in the same conversation in which he says, "The end is not yet." He is saying there is still a future, and things are still going to be happening, and some of those things will be of awesome portent. And he says, "Watch therefore . . . and be ready" (Matthew 24:42-44 RSV). In other words, *don't* live as though the interim is all there is. Anticipate that something else is going to happen. Don't consume all there is of today *today*; invest some of it in tomorrow; for tomorrow matters.

Jesus seems to be saying that, whatever else we may do today, the most important thing is to get ready for tomorrow, that, important as today is, tomorrow will be infinitely more so. He seems to be saying that out yonder ahead of us is something of ultimate

importance, something so very important that
everything this side of it is prelude. Profoundly aware
of this, Tennyson wrote of
One God, one law, one element,
And one far-off divine event,
To which the whole creation moves.
Between now and then we live in the interim; we are
going on to something. We need to master the art of
living *until.*

And speaking of this art, the first thing I would say
about it is this: Understand that what is finally going
to be the only important thing is surely the most
important thing all along the way. This, I believe, is
what Jesus is saying when he says, "Be ready." Be
now in a state of readiness for what will happen then.

The onward movement of our living is a perpetual
encounter with facts which become more and more
final. In our lives things are changing, and they are
going to change; they will not remain forever as they
are now. And the changes are impelling us in one
certain direction, funneling us on toward one specific
point, bringing us irrespressibly to one final fact.

There is a very pointed parable in Jeremiah 12:5:
"If you have run with footmen and they have wearied
you, then how can you race against horses? If in a land
of peace you have fallen down, then how will you do
when the Jordan overflows?" (K.J. adapted) Taking
Jeremiah's metaphor of the overflowing river, let us
see how things change as the river overflows. Let us
devise our own parable of the ingredients he gives us
here.

Here is farmer Jones with his family. They live on
a prosperous river farm, and it's a pleasant stream. In
its crystal water in summer they fish and swim, and in
winter they ice-skate on its surface. Along its banks
they picnic and play, and at its edge their livestock is
watered. It's a good life they live with the friendly
river.

And then comes the rain, and this is good. The grass will grow and the flowers will bloom, and the bottomlands will be coated with rich new soil as the water rises. But this time the rains keep coming, and the river keeps rising. The lower roads are closed. School has been dismissed, and the children are at home, and it's a festive time. There is all the excitement of a big show as the water covers the tops of the fence posts, and the children excitedly say, "See how high it is!"

There is an air of excited emergency, with adventure and dramatic activity. Save the haystack! get the pigs out of the lower barn! and the machinery out of the shed. Then — there is a slow dawning of truth, and the festive mood turns into crisis. After the lower barn has washed away and then the upper barn, and the rain is still falling, and the water is still rising and stands five feet deep on the living room floor, and the house shakes and trembles, and the family are all huddled upstairs, and the children are crying, then somehow the haystack and the pigs and the barns — they just don't seem to matter anymore. The issue is stripped to its bare essential: how to survive alive, how to keep the family from drowning. And then the worst comes; with an ominous grinding of timbers, the house shatters and falls apart, and each person is cast into the flood, alone, and the tide rolls over, and — darkness comes.

What is important then? When nothing is ahead except eternity, when all else is past and gone? The pleasant river, the picnic spot, the barns, the pigs, the house, and all the people — what is important then? When the river overflows? And, my dear friend, it will.

Curious, isn't it, how our estimate of values rises and falls according to circumstance. What we saw as of no value yesterday may grow in importance until it is all-important tomorrow. What was of great worth yesterday may fade today and be gone tomorrow. At age thirty one may have a consuming sex interest, but after living eighty or ninety years, somehow that part of life doesn't matter so much any more! At forty one may have a mammoth money interest, but when within three days of dying from cancer, money doesn't matter nearly as much as it once did.

For the child it's the bright toy to hold and manipulate and cuddle and use. But time passes, and the toy is put on the shelf, or packed in an old trunk, or thrown out with the rubbish. And then it's bright clothes, the exciting date, the fast car, the latest pop singer, school. But time passes, and school is over, the date becomes a marriage, and there is a home, and work to be done. It's the economic struggle, the security battle, the social circle, responsibility, deadlines. But time passes, and work is finished. Old friends, one by one, slip away, and the world looks strange, and it's the struggle to be occupied, to maintain identity, to keep alive. But time passes, and strength wanes, eyesight fails, footsteps falter, breath shortens, the heart flutters, familiar objects grow dim and seem to float away and away — and the river overflows.

One by one the great importances of other days have dwindled into insignificance. Only one consideration is left, one passionate hope: to hear One who said this long ago say it again, "Today you shall be with me in Paradise." You see, when Jesus said, "Be ready," he fully understood what life is like and how the course of life runs.

Life is a process of diminishing alternatives. We start out with many options; open doors are everywhere; we choose among many roads. And the roads merge and diverge across the landscape of years, and out there somewhere is a narrow passage into which all roads converge at last, a narrow place which all must pass. We talk sometimes about "situation ethics," but the time will come when this will not be a question for debate. It will be answered; there will be no situation to debate about.

As we try to determine how life ought to be lived, so many issues appear to be so relative. "It all depends," we say. How an issue looks may very well depend upon the light in which we see it. And remember this: grotesque distortions can be produced by lighting effects! But one day all our playing with the lights will be finished, and we shall see everything as it is. And this will include our view of God. As it is written, "We shall see him as he is" (1John 3:2). And, in the light of him, we shall see ourselves as we are. Perhaps this is what judgment is.

But we are now living in the meanwhile. That time has not yet come. The end is not yet. And I am saying to you that the first requirement for mastering the art of living until is to find out what will be at last the only important thing and make this the most important thing in your life *all along the way.*

Now, my friend, all of this may come through to you as a gloomy and uninspiring prospect, the prospect of diminishing alternatives as the roads of life converge upon the narrow place. But we are not stopping here. This is only the first of the things we need to understand about the art of living until. We go on now to look beyond the narrow place. And, even over there, we can hear the word of Jesus, "The end is not yet."

What is life? Well, whatever else it may be, it is certainly a-going-somewhere. And, for those of us who find our way, it is a going somewhere *good*, and when you are going to a good place, yes, you may enjoy the journey, but the best thing about it is getting there, reaching the goal. Who wants to be forever traveling and never arriving? The only way to get anywhere is at last to leave the traveled roads behind you.

Suppose you take a map of America and choose a

wonderful place you want to go, a place a long way off. There are many roads. In the beginning of your journey you may choose this way or that. But **every time you pass another intersection there are fewer remaining intersections to choose between.** The farther you go, the more and more you are committed, focused in upon that distant destination. And so it is until at last you turn into home stretch road, and round a curve, and the gates open, and you are there. And this is good.

More than anything else, it is the character of the destination which gives quality to the journey. Let us illustrate it this way: Highway 296 is a three-hundred-mile length of typical mid-western road. It is springtime, and driving along its distance, a forty-year-old man is going west. His destination is a hospital morgue where he will identify and claim the body of his beloved wife, her life lost earlier today in a grisley auto crash. The traveler sees nothing but a blurred view of highway pavement and roadside signs.

On the same day on the same road, another man is also driving west. Beside him sits his wife, and together they are on their way to the college campus where their beautiful daughter will graduate tomorrow with the highest honors the school can bestow. They see every lovely thing; for four years they have often traveled this road, but it's never been more thrilling or more delightful than it is today. You see, it's the destination that makes the difference.

I said a moment ago that all of us must pass the narrow place. But I did say *pass*, didn't I? And this is exactly what we do — pass it, and go on. Understand this, my dear Christian friend, we know where we are going.

A generation or two ago, Robert G. Ingersoll was a brilliant lecturer in America. An outspoken critic of the Bible and of the Christian Faith, one of his favorite platform performances was to lambast religion. On one occasion he said, "Someone will ask me whence I came and whither I am going. I do not know whence I came and I do not know whither I am going. I am on a wide sea sailing on a great ship. I know only a few of the passengers, and I have no acquaintance with either the pilot or the captain. If the ship goes down in mid-ocean, I will go down with it; but if it rounds into a beautiful harbor, I'll be there."

This bit of cynical oratory by Ingersoll evoked an inspiring response from A. B. Leonard, a Christian minister and man of faith. The response goes as follows: "If you ask me whence I came and whither I am going, I answer: I came from a God-created race that came out of the garden of Eden, and I am going to a City whose builder and maker is God. I, too, am sailing on a great ship, the old ship of Zion. I am acquainted with many of the passengers, and they are splendid people. But best of all, I am acquainted with the Pilot and the Captain, Jesus my Lord. This ship will not go down in mid-ocean, but will round into a beautiful harbor, and all on board will sing."

Well, here we have two ways of traveling, two ways of moving from where we are to the distant harbor. One way is the way of uncertainty, doubtful if a harbor exists. The other way is the way of assurance, certain of safe arrival and that the harbor is a happy place. And this, I think, is the second requirement in mastering the art of living until: Be confident of the outcome.

No, we cannot be sure what storms may set upon us along the way, but we can be sure of a safe haven at last. As the persecutions were tightening about the Apostle Paul, he left Ephesus to go to Jerusalem. In his farewell to the Ephesian Christians, he said, "And now, behold, I am going to Jerusalem, bound in the Spirit, not knowing what shall befall me there" (Acts 20:22 R.S.V.). As Paul saw it, Jerusalem was a part of the interim, not the end of the line. His faith reached far beyond Jerusalem and anything that might happen there. Later, writing from a Roman prison, he expressed that faith this way: "I know whom I have believed, and am certain that he is able to keep until that day that which I have entrusted to him" (2 Timothy 1:12 Ad.). Paul is saying: I do not know about Jerusalem, but I do know for sure about something farther along.

Many of the parables of Jesus are teaching us the crucial importance of having confidence in the outcome. One of these may be read in Luke 19. In this situation Jesus was dealing with a bunch of people who wanted everything to come out right — right then. They really believed, so it is written, that the Kingdom of God was to appear immediately. So Jesus told them a story to illustrate the importance of holding on, and keeping faith, and waiting it out, and seeing it through.

He said that a nobleman went into a far country to receive kingly power and then return. For the duration of his absence the nobleman put his affairs into the hands of ten trusted servants. His mission to the far country was a hazardous one, for some people hated him and said, "We do not want this man to reign over us." In the minds of some, apparently, the outcome of his mission was gravely in doubt.

Nine of his ten trusted servants believed in him, and while he was away they handled his affairs well. But the tenth servant, as he later confessed, was afraid. And he did not serve the nobleman well. In fact he didn't serve him at all. He took the money which had been entrusted to him and hid it in the ground; he buried it. In due course the nobleman returned, victorious, successful, and now a king. When he asked that servant for an accounting, all he got was a confession, an embarrassed apology for having done nothing.

"Why?" asked the king. "Why did you not do something?" And the man answered, "I was afraid."

Well, what was he afraid of? His assignment had been to take care of things for the prince until he should return, to act in the name of his lord, to look out for his interests during the interim of his absence. But the man was a victim of a paralyzing fear. He was afraid of how things might turn out. He was afraid that in the intrigue of king-making the enemies of the prince might undo him. He was afraid that the prince might lose his bid for kingly power. And this terrified tenth servant just didn't want to be identified with a lost cause.

So he hid his lord's money in the ground, pretended it wasn't there, and went about saying, I'm neutral in this matter. He wouldn't commit himself. He didn't believe strongly enough in the prince. Afraid of what might happen out yonder somewhere, he mismanaged the meanwhile. And having goofed up his interim assignment, when the prince returned in all his regal splendor, this poor fellow didn't get appointed to rule over any cities. The others did, but not this one. He failed in the interim; he didn't even get to the final test — and the way it turned out, there wasn't a final test anyway; the prince was a winner. But this poor fear-filled fellow didn't make it that far; when the victory came, he wasn't there to enjoy it. For him, alas, the interim proved more perilous than the event would ever have been. If only he could have believed — and acted accordingly! But he didn't believe; and he didn't act; and he failed. And he failed because he was afraid, afraid of the outcome.

I say to you, my dear friend, that one of the secrets of living in the interim is to believe in the outcome, how things will come out, how the interim will end. This parable of the mistrusting servant is one of the most directly revelant of all the parables of Jesus. In this parable he is speaking to us right where we are, right here in this interim where we live. And he is saying: You occupy until I come.

The fearful servant in the parable was not ready for his lord's return. He had not used the interim well, and he was gravely embarrassed when the prince reappeared — in the full glory of kingly might and authority. Well, in Matthew 24:44 Jesus lets us know what all of this means for us right here in our situation and condition. He says, "Therefore you also must be ready; for the Son of man is coming at an hour you do not expect."

And he says, "Watch therefore" (Matthew 24:42). In the New English Bible this verb is translated "keep awake." Be alert. Be on your toes. Stand at attention. Fall in. Get with it. Some intervals are times for sleeping, but not this one. This one is a time for watchfulness.

This, it seems to me, is the third requirement for mastering the art of living until: keep awake. The Apostle Paul was quite interim-conscious when he wrote to the Thessalonian church, "You yourselves know very well that the Day of the Lord will come as unexpectedly as a thief comes in the night. When people say, 'There is peace and security,' then destruction will come upon them . . . But you are not in darkness, brethren, for that Day to surprise you like a thief. For you are all children of light, and of the day; we are not of the night or of darkness. So then let us not sleep, as others do, but let us keep awake and be sober" (1 Thessalonians 5:2-6).

Paul apparently wishes us to understand what kind of interim this is in which we are living. It is a kind which demands alertness, attention, activity. There may be a kind of interim which is simply a waiting period, but this one isn't. He who would live it well isn't just a waiter; he is also a worker. He foresees that out yonder somewhere is something he must be ready for, and he is working on it. He believes in a gloriously wonderful eventuation of things, and he is working toward it. He hears Jesus say, "Occupy until I come," and he is therefore occupied.

Someone wrote concerning a certain woman: "Fourscore years this life she led: in the morning she arose, and at night went to bed." What a career! Day-to-day existence; alive, perhaps, at least biologically, but not living. No sense of interim occupancy. A man who had retired from his lifetime employment had obviously also retired from living, for when someone asked him how he spent his time, he replied, "I get up in the morning, put on my robe and slippers, make my way to the front door, pick up the morning newspaper, bring it into the house, and turn to the obituary section to see if my name is there, and if it isn't, I go back to bed!" Well, that sort of "life style" doesn't really qualify as living. Surely it doesn't qualify as living *until* — anything. There isn't much affirmative expectancy in it; it's without point or purpose, a daily survival, with an attitude of indifference even toward that.

Some years ago Archibald Rutledge, traveling on a Southern river boat, observed the exceptional cleanliness of the craft. The deck was immaculate, the brass gleaming in the sun, everything spotless. This state of affairs being quite unusual on such boats, Mr. Rutledge sought out the big black engineer, whose responsibility included overall care of the boat, and asked him why this particular one was so remarkably clean. The smilingly-proud caretaker replied, "You see, sir, I've got a glory." And, my dear friend, we should have one, too. Our glory, very much like his, should be to add a radiance to all that is around us. No, not necessarily by polishing brass and scrubbing floors, although that may well be a part of it, but chiefly by encouraging and engendering spiritual vitality and moral beauty in all we touch.

Let me repeat it: The interim we occupy is not just a waiting period; it is a working time. Verse 46 of the 24th chapter of Matthew, loosely translated, reads: "Blessed is that servant whom his master, when he comes, will find *doing something!*" Jesus goes on to suggest that the interim-occupying servant may fail because he grows weary of waiting. And it's no great wonder that he grows weary if he is doing nothing but wait. Jesus even says the faltering servant may say to himself, "My master delays his coming," and may therefore begin to "beat his fellow servants and to eat and drink with the drunken" (Matthew 24:49). Well, it's the classic expression of boredom — to behave this way. And haven't we seen a lot of it in our time? A good healthy interest in doing something worthwhile is the very best preventive medicine for this kind of frustration. Your day is always a shorter one if you're busy.

And it's not only shorter; it's also better. If you are pleasantly employed doing something you really believe in, how time flies! There just isn't time to get bored and beat up on anybody, and neither the time nor the inclination to contribute yours to the regiment of elbows lined up on the counter of the town bar. Jesus knew what he was talking about. And he goes on to say that the master of that delinquent servant will come on a day when he is not expected and will punish him "and put him with the hypocrites" (Matthew 24:50-51). Well, maybe that's where he belongs — with the hypocrites. For he was taking up space in an interim that he really didn't occupy, standing in shoes he really didn't fill.

In the second Epistle of Peter, there is a discussion of life in this interim, and there is the assertion that, after a long time has gone by, some people will be scoffers, saying, "Where is the promise of his coming? For ever since the fathers fell asleep, all things have continued as they were" (3:4). Apparently these people, bored with waiting, have concluded that the interim is all there'll ever be. They seem to hold the view that because things have "continued as they were," they will always do that. These people seem to reason that since the Lord has not come, therefore, he won't. And what an amazing piece of logic is this! Where is the promise of his coming? I can tell you exactly where it is — out there ahead of us, somewhere. It's there at the end of the interim, wherever that is. And we are living in *time until*.

Jesus compares our time with the time before the great flood. Says he, "As were the days of Noah, so will be the coming of the Son of man. For as in those days before the flood they were eating and drinking, marrying and giving in marriage, until the day when Noah entered the ark, and they did not know until the flood came and swept them all away, so will be the coming of the Son of man." The people of Noah's time were preoccupied with their interim, and they got lost in it. Not only were they not working, they weren't even waiting. Put in the modern vernacular, they were "living it up." Actually, that phrase is a good one, very descriptive. There is some question about the "living" part of it, but no question about the "up" part. They were using up their interim. And then suddenly they discovered it was all gone. They had used it as though it was all there would ever be, but it wasn't; there was also something called a flood, and they weren't prepared for that. Noah was, but they weren't. Getting lost in the interval, they drowned in the flood with which it ended.

For centuries prior to the birth of Jesus, the Jewish people looked for the coming of the Messiah. But at length when he appeared, most did not understand that this was he. Somehow during the long wait their eye for seeing the miracle of him became clouded, and it is one of the strange anomalies of history that when he came they never really comprehended who he was.

From that interval prior to his first appearing, the prophet Habakkuk speaks a word of counsel and guidance which has a powerful meaning for us in this interval prior to his next appearing. The word is: "The vision awaits its time; it hastens to the end — it will not lie. If it seem slow, wait for it; it will surely come" (Habakkuk 2:3 R.S.V.). For us in our day, this is a beautiful expression of the faith we live by. Where is the promise of his coming? Out there ahead somewhere — and you can count on that.

For long centuries before Jesus was born there was a looking forward, and anticipation. For the fulfillment of hope and dream, faith was pointing into the future. Then came Christ. He came proclaiming the Kingdom of God. He came with the promise of peace, of the triumph of right, the vindication of truth, the coronation of beauty.

Now, again, for the fulfillment of the promise, faith is pointing forward. Our hopes are for a time that is yet to be. But the time is not yet. We have assurance that the "Day of the Lord" will come. But that day has not yet come. In our time we live in the interim — until. How far we have come into the interim we do not know, nor do we know how far we have yet to go.

Often we pray The Lord's Prayer, and we say, "Thy Kingdom come, thy will be done." We send our prayer up to God out of a world where brutality and selfishness are common, where the rape of the good and the prostitution of the holy are everywhere apparent. We send our prayer up to God out of a world where some people despise other people because of the color of their skin or the accent with which they pronounce their names, out of a world where the human spirit is so much ravished by hate and cynicism and greed. And we say, "Thy will be done." But it isn't yet.

The question is: How are we to live in the meanwhile? What is our insight for living *until*? Question: Until the final vindication of right and truth, how do we deal with them? Answer: Just as though that vindication were achieved already. Question: Until the final judgment of values, how do we measure them? Answer: As though that judgment were made already. Question: Until the ultimate triumph of Christ, how do we relate to him? Answer: As though he were the victor now, for indeed he is. Question: Until the final resolution of the struggle between good and evil, where should we stand in the conflict? Answer: In the best light we have, in the posture of faith, in the stance of the overcomer, for the triumph of the good is as sure as though it had happened yesterday.

I am trying to say that a faith and conviction and a pattern and a way of life for the interim is one that keeps the eventual end in view, believes in it firmly, is committed to it implicitly, and trusts the outcome completely. And this faith is one that can endure the uncertainty, the insecurity, and the unknown for a while. Let's put it this way: When *what is* is uncertain, then live by what is *certain to be.*

There will be a tomorrow. And against the clouded backdrop of today, I offer you a gift for it. I don't apologize for being a minister of the best there is in the world, or for trying to minister it to you. In Romans, chapter one, the Apostle Paul describes conditions of murder, deceit, immorality, tribulation, and anguish. But over against all of this he confidently sets the power of the Christian gospel, writing in this same chapter: "I am not ashamed of the gospel of Christ, for it is the power of God unto salvation" (1:16).

After the atomic age began, one of the scientists on the team which made the first bomb said, "We scientists have looked into the mouth of hell, and we are afraid." A minister of the Christian gospel commented: "For centuries we ministers have been dealing with the deep, dark problems of humankind; we have long been accustomed to looking into the mouth of hell, and we are *not* afraid."

An apocalypse is a picture of the end. We have two apocalypses which are commonly viewed in our time. First there is the scientific or secular apocalypse. It portrays an irreversible deterioration of things, a mushroom-shaped cloud above the earth, oxygen depleted from the air, the ozone layer destroyed, the earth bombarded with burning rays under which no living thing can survive — and no hope.

Secondly, there is the Christian apocalypse, vividly, symbolically, and dramatically portrayed as elements melting with fervent heat, rocks falling, the sun darkened, the moon turned to the color of blood, all things dissolving, and an angel standing with one foot on land and one on sea proclaiming that "time shall be no more" (Revelation 10:5,6 K.J.V.).

Well, choose your apocalypse. One is about as dismal as the other, except that there is an additional element in that second picture, one which does not appear in the first. In the midst of melting elements, falling rocks, blood-colored moon, and all things dissolving, there emerges a powerful additional dimension of the picture. In the midst of the ruin and desolation, the mighty Christ stands forth, the world's incomparable Redeemer. He arises out of the shambles, triumphant and victorious — and his people are with him. They are the "called, and chosen, and faithful" (Revelation 17:14). With him "they shall reign forever and ever" (Revelation 22:5). It is with this gargantuan trumpeting of glorious promise that our Holy Bible sweeps to its majestic conclusion; here on this note of redemption the Book closes.

So I think I will choose the Christian apocalypse, the one which has redemption in it. The late great historian Arnold Toynbee made this same choice. In his monumental work, *A Study of History*, Professor Toynbee describes the barbarian overthrow of the Byzantine Empire. In A.D. 711 Emperor Justinian II was preparing to flee for his life. But the empress said to her husband: "You may flee if you like; the ship is in the harbor, and the wind is in the sail; but as for me I prefer to remain and die with the empire, because empire makes a fine winding-sheet." Toynbee's comment is this: "When I read that, I thought: a finer winding-sheet is the Kingdom of God, for that is one from which there is a resurrection."

No, my friend, I do not know what will happen in our world, or to me, tomorrow. But I don't have to know; for God is safe to trust. As someone has said, "I do not know what the future holds, but I know who holds the future." I know to whom time belongs in the long run; who holds the future — at the last. So the gift I would give you for tomorrow is not a *foresight* to determine what will happen when, for that would solve nothing; but it is an *insight* for whatever may happen anytime, and this solves everything.

Often asked is the question: Why do I suffer this or that? The question is unanswerable really. But here I would offer an insight which makes the unanswerable question unnecessary. Over against all the fear there is in the world let me set one firm fact. Right will win, truth will last, beauty shall be eternal. In the eventuation of things, all is well for what is good. All which is this side of that is interim, and only the interim is uncertain. And if we can have faith for the eventuation, we can have power for the interim.

To us who walk with Christ in this world, trials will come; but we can overcome, because we are certain of the outcome. We can go through almost anything if we can be sure of something beyond it. And we can be. There may be a Calvary, but it is endurable if we can be sure of the Easter which follows. God will not be defeated; he will not abandon his people or his world to any devil. We see this in the resurrection of Christ. We hear it in the words of Jesus, "Because I live you shall live also" (John 14:19). We observe it in the witness of Paul: "I know whom I have believed, and

am sure that he is able to keep that which I have
committed to him" (2 Timothy 1:12).

We need to hear the word of Jesus, "When you
hear of commotions and wars and rumors of wars,
remember that the end is not yet." Believe this; know
it; hold it firmly; never let it go. Present conditions
may speak with all the noise of great thunder, but
they do not speak the final word. Here is the ultimate
meaning of faith. It puts us in relation to the
finalization of things, sets our life in right relation with
all that is and is to be.

What does it all mean? I think it means: Line up
with life and with God; get on the side of the universe;
join the triumphant; get with the winner; for every
good and beautiful thing is on the way up and on, and
every evil and ugly thing is on the way down and out.
How long the way we do not know; but we don't have
to know. It is not an empty phrase when Jesus says, "I
am the way, the truth, and the life" (John 14:6).

This Faith called Christian is not merely isolated
spurts of believing this or that, but it is a long-term
confidence in the dependability of God, and in the
eternal character of right and truth and beauty. And
this confidence is our strength for living; it is our faith
for both working and resting. In our working we can
know that every good effort becomes a part of an
ultimate victory. In our resting we can know there is a
place to let down with confidence.

Dr. George MacDonald told of a fox hunt in which
the hounds pursued their prey until he climbed to a
high ledge overlooking the valley below. As the hounds
noisily followed his trail up the steep mountainside,
there in the beaming sun, on the ledge just outside his
den, sat the great red fox quietly licking a paw. Dr.
MacDonald made the point: If you have a sure refuge
into which you know you can go, the noisy braying of
the hounds of life really doesn't worry you much. And
his point was well made. This kind of faith brings

power, because we know that finally there is nothing to be afraid of. And it brings joy, because we know that now, and ultimately also, there is everything to live for.

Far out in the wilds, a woodsman came upon half-a-dozen boys in Scout uniform. "Are you lost?" he asked them. And they answered, "We don't know where we are, but we're not lost; we are with the scoutmaster, and he knows the way home." Well, friend, you and I may not know exactly where we are either — in this interval, this interim, this interlude, this meanwhile. But if we are with the Master, we can trust him to know the way home. No, the end is not yet; but whatever it is, and whenever it comes, this is the Faith that will hold us until it does.

Your Image of Tomorrow

Matthew 3:1-12
"He who is coming after me . . ."

"Among those who are born of women . . ." If you are
thinking of the human race, this is a rather inclusive
statement; I can't think of very many people it leaves
out! And this is a statement of Jesus as he offers a
summa cum laude of highest praise to one of his
associates in the dissemination of truth and light. He
says, "Among those who are born of women, there has
not arisen a greater prophet than John the Baptizer"
(Matthew 11:11; Luke 7:28).

What was it that was so great about John — this son
of Zacharias and Elizabeth, this leather-clad,
locust-eating rustic from the "hill country" of Judea?
Actually, it seems to me, aspects of greatness were
breaking out all over this man, the prophet who stands at
this end of a long line of prophets. They had spoken
hopefully and longingly of the coming of the Messiah, but
to John the lot fell to introduce him to the world. So,
yonder beside Israel's historic Jordan, John said,
"World, may I present my cousin, your Savior?"

Surely it is a high privilege to make a presentation of
this kind, a privilege which, incidentally, nobody but
John has ever had. Doing this, however, does not
necessarily require any large measure of greatness. But
John did something else which does; he said another
thing which only the great can ever say. Concerning the
Messiah, he said, "One is coming after me; he is mightier
than I; I am unworthy of him; I am simply helping to
prepare the way for him."

It was an aspect of John's greatness that he could see
himself as who he was, as standing where he stood. With
no tinge of bitterness or jealousy or self-pity, he could
say concerning Jesus, "He must increase, but I must

decrease." (John 3:30) He could see his own star eclipsed by the brighter sun, and could turn with upreached arms to welcome that more brilliant light. "Little" people usually do not make good forerunners. Most of us, of course, are forerunners of something or other; but generally we don't know it at the time. John knew that he was, and he was willing to be. He was content to draw aside the curtain, focus the spotlight upon Another, and then step back into the shadows. There are dimensions of greatness in the character of anyone who can do that as gracefully and graciously as did John.

In the story of *Adam Bede*, George Eliot describes a certain conceited person as being "like the cock who thought the sun had risen to hear him crow." I've known, as you probably have, a few persons along the way who were just about as vain as this. Remember that line by Tennyson: "One far-off divine event to which the whole creation moves?" I knew one fellow once who apparently believed himself to be that divine event. He seemed to have the idea that all of time and circumstance, up to then, had conspired to accomplish only one purpose, and that was just to get him into the world. He saw himself as creation's ultimate achievement, the apex toward which all else had forever been aimed, and beyond which nothing of any notable quality would ever appear again. There isn't much future in that.

This man John was a different type; beyond himself he saw something else, something better, something to be cherished and looked forward to. "He who is coming after me is mightier than I," says he. It is he, not I, who will do the wonderful things the world needs to have done, he says. "His winnowing fork is in his hand," and he will put everything where it belongs; he will set things right. John had a hope, an expectation. He had an outlook. In other words, he could see out. And the view was forward. He could see beyond himself, and beyond his day; and what he saw was good.

John had a vision of the future, an image of tomorrow; and in the midst of that picture stood hope and redemption and rightness. What he saw in his image of tomorrow gave him courage to stand by the Jordan and challenge his world from its lowest peasant to its highest king. He stood in the finest tradition of the Hebrew prophets of the Eternal, and like all who had come and gone before him, it was in the light of what he saw in his image of tomorrow that he saw the moral squalor of his own day. The beauty and glory of what he saw ahead of him rendered intolerable the ugliness of what he saw around him. And so in Israel another prophet's heart was stirred and another prophet's voice was heard. And Jesus said he was the greatest of them all.

Well, my dear friend, here we are today, you and I. What about tomorrow? What is your image of it? Do you have an OUT-look? What is it? As you look out from within, what is it you see? What do you see out there ahead of you? In my theological school days I sat in classes taught by Professor Earl Marlatt, who wrote what in my opinion is one of the finest Christian hymns ever written by anybody. This prayer-hymn, starting as life starts, petitions:

Spirit of Life, in this new dawn,
Give us the faith that follows on . . .

Then as the hymn reaches its end, climaxing as life does, it offers this prayer:

Give us thy vision, eyes that see,
Beyond the dark, the dawn and Thee . . .

These we need, you and I: the faith that follows on and the vision that sees beyond.

Let us unite our minds, then, to think together a little about your image of tomorrow.

In Berkeley, California, a few years ago a blind comptometer operator stood at a busy street corner, waiting in the hope that some kind person would assist her to cross. Sensing a presence beside her, she said, "Please, may I go across with you?" A man's voice replied, "I'll be glad if you will." Arm in arm the two walked across the street together. When safely on the other side, the man said, "Thank you; when one has been blind as long as I have, he appreciates a favor like this!" Both were blind, and neither knew the other was.

Well, moving into the future as we all are, we are all blind. We are blind not because we have no vision, but because as yet there is nothing there to see; it hasn't happened yet; it hasn't materialized or taken shape. But inevitably we form some image of what it's going to be like, and we "see" it this way or we "see" it that way. And we are talking about a most important subject when we speak of our images of tomorrow.

They can be quite unlike what tomorrow eventually turns out to be. Often we are very unfair to the future. We mistrust it; we mangle it brutally even before it issues from the womb of time. We borrow troubles that haven't come yet; we wear ourselves away worrying about problems that will never be. How often we have crossed perilous old bridges long before we ever got to them, and in the after-years, having passed them, we have looked back and said, "Really, they weren't actually all that bad."

Have you seen ancient maps of unexplored portions of the world? Maps that portrayed the prevailing ideas of what lay beyond, the untraveled lands and the uncrossed seas? Maps from before the adventures of Marco Polo and Christopher Columbus and Ferdinand Magellan ? How grotesquely inaccurate those maps were! How vastly they differed from what the explorer eventually found! How fantastic were the notions the ancients had about what was out there — a dropping-off-place, mammoth sea serpents to swallow up ships. But as things turned out, it wasn't that way at all. You know, if Columbus had believed half the maps and legends of his time he would never have lifted an anchor!

Well, we are all traveling into the unexplored land, and we ought to be careful how we map it until we've traveled there. Certainly we shouldn't let the future do things to us it never meant to do. It is my faith that the future means to be friendly; and I don't thnk we ought to treat it as an enemy. If we do, and start in to do battle with it, I can tell you this: It's a battle we can never win. Let's not suspect it of standing over us with a club waiting for a chance to clobber us into the ground, or of lurking in the shadows to pounce upon us around the next dark corner.

And surely we shouldn't be afraid of the future — not if we are Christians. I am hearing Jesus say, "I am the way." And he is talking about himself, and about you, and about your future, and about your journey into it. He is saying that he is the way all the way through, beyond whatever it is, even beyond death — and especially beyond it. Yes, some days will be darker than others — which means, of course, that the others will be brighter. Were this not so we couldn't make the comparison in the first place, could we? In the conflict between our future-related hopes and fears, we must keep our hopes in control, and we can if we are walking into tomorrow hand in hand with one who is going on. He isn't going to drop our hand out there somewhere and say, "So long; it was nice to have you walk with me; but this is as far as we go."

When I was calling on him in a hospital, a good man said to me, "I am not afraid of dying." And I said to him, "Why should you be? For, after all, if you are walking with your hand in our Lord's hand, after you have died your hand will still be in his." Often in hospital rooms I have had occasion to say, "Every day is a good day when you are going in the right direction." And it is.

As we think of our future-related fears and hopes, let us not overlook the immense importance of another and even greater future-related reality: our Faith. No, I am fully aware that even by faith we cannot yet see what will happen tomorrow; but if we live by faith, we do not have to see; because if we live by faith, we have an advantage better than seeing *what* is in the future; we know *who* is there, and we can trust him.

Remember Abraham? He was called to go into a land that God would show him. Abraham did not know where he was going; but he knew with whom, and this was enough.

I suppose there are two ways of walking into tomorrow. Let me illustrate. I saw two blind men, each walking along the main street of town. One groped his way, arms outstretched in wild motions of search, his feet shuffling tentatively as though they mistrusted one another. The other man strode, a spring in his step, white cane tapping lightly before him as he went, his body erect, head held high in the posture of one who sees. The first man is so afraid of stumbling that he never walks; he only gropes. The other is so in love with walking that a stumble for him will be only a very small thing. And both will stumble sometimes. The difference is that one will do it with fear and dread, and between stumbles will grope, and the other will do it without fear, and between stumbles will walk.

In some ways all of us are like blind men moving into the future, and we have the choice between being gropers and walkers. You can wear yourself away worrying whether, with your next step, your foot will land on a banana peel — when as a matter of fact there may not be a banana peel anywhere within a thousand city blocks. Did you hear about the mother bear that was teaching her cubs to walk? One said, "Momma, which foot shall we put forward first?" and she growled, "Shut up and walk!" That's pretty good advice, really. The centipede would soon go crazy with frustration if he should start worrying about which of his one hundred feet to pick up next and exactly where to put it down.

We all live by some image of tomorrow. What's yours? I am saying to you: No matter what the circumstances, how old you are, the condition of your fortune or health, if you are walking with the Lord of life, you can walk into tomorrow with confidence and hope, and nothing is there to be afraid of. Yes, I know that we should walk with due caution, be alert for dangers; there are stumbling blocks we must try to avoid, perilous precipices we might fall over. A normal part of walking is to use whatever vision we have. We ought to walk in the best light we can get, use discernment in choosing the roads and pursuing the goals which arise before us.

Have you seen a beautiful little thing called *The Hummel Book*, paintings and drawings by a wonderful Catholic sister named Berta Hummel and verses by an equally wonderful Viennese lady named Margarete Seemann? Directed to children mostly, the volume gives us this little verse:

Carry your candle with care, my child!
The wind is waiting,
The wind is waiting to blow it out.

Now I fully agree that one should be wary of the waiting wind, and I know that winds are waiting. But I would make this point: If you are too apprehensive about the wind, you will *never light your candle in the first place* — and that, I think, would be more calamitous than to risk it to the wind. Yes, we are all going on into tomorrow; we have no choice. So light your candle and venture into the wind. It might be a gentle zephyr, or it might be a stormy gale; for life has some of both. But your Christ is the Master of the raging winds, and he is Lord, and they are not.

There is at least one very important difference between a painting and a photograph. The photograph is an actual reproduction of a scene; the painting is the artist's interpretation or impression of it. The photograph is a record of what is actually there; the painting is what the artist sees as being there. Of course we have no technique by which we can photograph the future. You cannot photograph what isn't there, and the future isn't — yet. But we can certainly paint pictures of the future; and we do; we do it all the time. You look into the future and paint a picture on the canvas of your mind. The picture may be clear or dim, bright or dark, inviting or forbidding; or it may be a mixture of elements; but, whatever the quality of your artistry, you are making some kind of image of tomorrow.

In our representation of the future, we are painters rather than photographers. We form our impressions of what we think things will be like, and we do not so much live by tomorrow's reality as we do by our impression of what that reality will be. As a matter of fact, we of the human family are a great bunch of picture painters.

Not only do we paint our impressions of the future, but also the current realities of the world around us are likewise reproduced within us. For the most part, we live by the images we form, the pictures we make, the impressions we have — images, pictures, and impressions of people, places, things, events, relationships, motives, intentions, and of almost everything around us. A little data is fed into our consciousness, and inevitably we construct a picture around it. Unfortunately, our inward reproductions do not always conform to the outward reality; too much we paint distorted pictures; we give them the wrong coloring; we see in the scene not so much what is there, but what we want to see, or expect to, or have made up our minds we are going to. Such distorted images are a major source of much of the world's sorrow. It is of urgent importance that in all our picture-painting we represent the subject as faithfully as we can.

In no case, though, can a distorted image prove more devastating than when it is an image of tomorrow. Too often our images of tomorrow have huge, hairy, monstrous apparitions of fear prominent in the foreground or lurking somewhere in the shadows. A story is told about a man who was a successful bill collector. He could collect old debts from people upon whom all the other collectors had given up years before.

Someone asked him how he did it. He replied, "O, it's quite simple really. I just write them one letter, and in that letter I tell them just one thing, and that one thing is this: if you don't pay this bill immediately, that thing which you are afraid will happen will happen." He was, of course, gambling on the rather safe bet that most people have some fear of something in the future.

Then there is the story of the fellow on shipboard who was miserably seasick. One of his friends found him hanging over the ship's rail and said, "Cheer up, buddy; nobody ever died from being seasick." "Don't tell me that," said the poor, pallid victim with a groan, "it's only my hope of dying that's kept me alive so far." These two amusing stories have one thing in common: an anxiety concerning the future. And I strongly suspect that if you could add up all the anxiety which today indwells the minds and spirits of the human family, it would come to an imponderable total.

Once, on an airplane flying west, my mission somewhat sad and the outcome unsure, I found myself considering the others with me on the flight, some one hundred and eighty of them, all strangers to me. What would happen on arrival? Where would each go? What would each do? Each, in view of his own image of tomorrow, was living in his own world — and, without a doubt, there were about one hundred and eighty worlds on that plane, and probably no two of them alike.

Well, my friend, each of us is on an airplane flying west. Tomorrow will overtake us; we cannot outrace it. If our image of tomorrow is inviting, if it offers fulfillment of dream, then we can move toward it with eagerness and hope. If the image is foreboding, we are likely to move toward it with dread and fear. For most of us the tomorrows hold some of both — and our fears and our hopes are all intertwined and intermixed.

Permit me now to point out two problems common to most of us as we form our images of tomorrow. The first problem is that the image may be unclear, out of focus, confused, hazy. How often the wrongdoer will foolishly hope and the rightdoer will foolishly fear. I know that in saying this I imply a relationship between moral action and what tomorrow will bring. Well, there is — there is a realtionship. Evil, if it runs its full course, leads to ruin; goodness, maintained until the end, leads to glory. But frequently the wrongdoer hopes that his sin will not "find him out" (Numbers 32:23) — at least not yet anyway — and that he can get by with it for a while. And frequently the rightdoer fears that out yonder somewhere a storm may come or that around the next bend in the road some awesome peril may lurk unseen.

The other common problem with our image-making is that we do not view tomorrow as a long enough day, or, we do not consider enough tomorrows. There will be more than one, you know. Good people need to remember: "Though weeping endure for a night, joy comes in the morning." (Psalms 30:5) If on the first day Jesus is crucified, and on the second day his body is guarded in a sealed tomb, so what? — on the third day he will arise! You can count on it: there will be a third-day morning, a vindication of right and truth and beauty, a confirmation of love and an affirmation of power. And all of this is tomorrow, some tomorrow. I'm not sure that which one is of any great importance. Any one is good enough.

If you want a proper image of the future, then get all of it into your picture. In Luke 12:16-21 Jesus gives us the parable of a rich landowner whose lands one season brought forth so abundantly that his barns were too small for the harvest. He commanded his servants to tear them down and build larger barns. Then he spoke to his soul, and this is what he said: "Soul, you have much goods laid up for many years; take it easy; eat, drink, and be merry." The next voice we hear in the story is the voice of God, as God speaks to this man, saying, "You fool! Tonight your soul is required of you; and those things you have prepared, whose will they be?"

God didn't exactly mince words with this fellow. He really put it on the line for him. And right there in a few split seconds that farmer learned something which he hadn't thought much about before, if at all. He had looked ahead, and he had felt very secure with the bountiful harvest which had been his. He believed himself to be all fixed for as far as he could see. But with shocking suddenness he discovered that he hadn't seen as far as he should have. He had looked ahead for several years, considered himself provided for for "many days." But there was that other day which he hadn't seen. It hadn't been in his picture; it wasn't a part of his image of tomorrow. Perhaps we should call it the judgment day, for surely it was, for him, just that — judgment. He ran into something he hadn't reckoned with — the day when all things are put right; and he hadn't counted on that; he just hadn't figured it in. He had framed his picture too narrowly, and what he had left out was what undid him.

Earlier I mentioned Dr. Marlatt's fine hymn, *Spirit of Life, in this New Dawn.* I mentioned the prayer with which the hymn concludes:

Give us thy vision, eyes that see,
Beyond the dark, the dawn and Thee.

I think this prayer has the approval of Jesus, and I base this on something he said to his disciples long ago. He had walked with them for many months, teaching them. He had exposed them to dimensions of life they hadn't known before; he had opened up for them ranges and reaches of life they hadn't known were there; he had disclosed vistas of the heights and depths of meaning which were new to them. And his disciples were impressed. They were seeing things they had never seen before, and, from the Gospel record, it is apparent that Jesus was pleased.

He drew his disciples aside and said to them privately, "Blessed are the eyes which see what you see! For I tell you that many prophets and kings desired to see what you see, and did not see it." (Luke 10:23 R.S.V.)

My message to you, dear friend, is a call to the far vision;
my prayer is that your eyes may be blessed in seeing.

Yonder at the western end of the Mediterranean,
where Europe and Africa almost touch, stands the
towering fourteen-hundred-foot mass of rock called
Gibraltar. The ancient people who lived along the
Mediterranean shores looked upon that rock as the end
of their world. Beyond it was a mystery, the awesome
and forbidding waters of the great sea of Atlas, the
Atlantic. High on the Rock of Gibraltar, so it is said,
someone chisled the Latin legend, *"Ne Plus Ultra,"*
meaning "Nothing More Beyond." Then one August day
in 1492 three small ships under command of Christopher
Columbus loosed from the port of Palos in Spain, swung
into the open sea, and with sails trimmed for sailing
west, disappeared into the sunset. After many months,
the adventuring explorer was back with glowing
accounts of other lands beyond the sea. And, so it is said,
someone altered the legend on the face of Gibraltar,
erasing the negative *"Ne"* and leaving only *"Plus Ultra,"*
meaning: "More Beyond."

And there is — there is more beyond. And I do not
mean geographically only. I mean that in terms of our
human life there is more beyond, vast areas which may
lie beyond the horizon of our natural sight, clothed in
mists and shadowed in mystery. And we do not have a
Columbus to venture forth and explore for us and return
and report to us. We just have to see. But there is much
we cannot see with the unaided eye alone. Neither is
there a powerful telescope which will help us here; but
there is the lens of faith. And he who sees with the aid of
this lens may clearly perceive what others miss.

Ann Sullivan Macy, the wonderful lady who, as the
teacher of Helen Keller, liberated this deaf and blind child
from the prison of her darkness, once spelled out this
message in her pupil's hand: "The best and most
beautiful things in the world cannot be seen or even
touched, but just felt in the heart."

We really haven't gotten perspective upon what life is all about until we have begun to see with the heart as well as the eye. The Apostle Paul is thinking of this fact in Ephesians 1:18 when he expresses the prayerful wish that we will have knowledge of God, as he says, "having the eyes of your hearts enlightened." The heart needs an enlightened eye. We need the heart as an instrument of vision, and it should be in good trim for seeing. The Authorized Version of our Bible translates this: "The eyes of your *understanding.*" We need to see with the understanding.

In this passage Paul is pointing to realities beyond which he fervently hopes we will comprehend, and by which we will be inspired and guided. Listen to what he is saying: "I remember you in my prayers, that the God of our Lord Jesus Christ, the Father of glory, may give you a spirit of wisdom and of revelation in the knowledge of him, having the eyes of your hearts enlightened, that you may know what is the hope to which he has called you, what are the riches of his glorious inheritance in the saints, and what is the immeasurable greatness of the power in us who believe . . ."

One of the afflictions which sometimes impairs the physical sense of sight is myopia, more commonly called near-sightedness. The myopiac cannot see very well very far. I have known a great many people who have suffered from a kind of psychological and spiritual myopia.

I read of a man who traveled around the world carrying with him a sophisticated camera equipped to take pictures at any distance from five feet to infinity. Throughout the entire journey he allowed the focus to remain set on five feet; and when he got home, the only clear pictures he had were those of objects just five feet away. What a waste! He might have photographed the Matterhorn with the sun rising over its summit, but he didn't. He might have gotten a spectacular picture of clouds over Mount Blanc, but he didn't. He might have returned with a beautiful view of the moon over the

Mediterranean, but he didn't. Well, you and I, my friend, are made to look into infinity, to view the unseen — and it is such a tragic waste when our focus is set on five feet and we never change it from that setting.

Once I saw a dozen vultures circling against a crimson sunset. Nature's evening pageantry was glorious, and my heart leaped within me as my whole being was infused with the beauty of that western sky. But I'm sure the vultures never saw it. Their poor pea-brains were set on the carcass of some dead thing on the ground. Of course, this is the nature of vultures. But it should never be the character of human beings to miss the glory for the carcass of some ugly thing. The prophet Jeremiah was sickened and saddened by the insensitivity of the people of his time. He cried out to them, "Hear this, O foolish and senseless people, who have eyes, but do not see, who have ears, but hear not." (Jeremiah 5:21)

I wonder what Jeremiah would say to us in our time. We tend to give higher priority to quantity than to quality. Someone has pointed out that the one word which has most aptly characterized us of Western Civilization in the twentieth century has been the word "more." Our prevailing aspirations are for more automobiles, TV sets, refrigerators, and all the vast repertoire of push-button gadgetry which has prompted someone to comment that "Our civilization is like a hardware store caught in a whirlwind." Speaking of the dimensions of our being, Jesus says, "You *are* more." But generally our larger interest is in *having* more; we are more concerned with having than being. We tend to have a greater interest in a kind of breadth than we have in any sort of depth. Our inclination is to take a quick glance at everything and a penetrating look at nothing. It may be an epitome of our time that when we are confronted with a problem, we assemble huge masses of statistics, feed them into a computer, and ask it to tell us what they mean!

46

Blessed are the eyes that see beyond — eyes of understanding, expectation, faith. During the first World War, Quentin Roosevelt, an American military pilot in Europe, and son of former President Theodore Roosevelt, was shot down in battle, and killed. His father wrote the inscription to mark his grave, and here is the inscription Theodore Roosevelt wrote: "he has outsoared the shadows of our night." It is, I think, the privilege of each of us to do that. In the ongoing process of our human living, shadows occur in many forms, and there are many kinds of night. Most of us who have lived very long can testify to the truth of this. But we will not be terrified by either the night or the shadows if we can have an image of tomorrow with enough brightness in it to drive the dark away.

Now let me say a rather important thing: It isn't always easy to have this kind of image. At any moment we must view the future from wherever we are; and we who are living in our day are looking into the future out of a terribly pessimistic time. Remember Jesus' parable of the prince, going to claim his kingdom, who turned over his affairs to his associates to care for them until he should return? Remember that one who failed so miserably? And do you remember why he failed? He said it himself, "I was afraid." He had been afraid the venture of the prince might not turn out well, and he wished not to be identified with a loser. He was afraid also, apparently, that if the prince did succeed and did indeed become a king, he might be a hard man to work for. So whether the prince's play for the throne proved successful or unsuccessful, this man could see only the problems. Either way, he looked on the dark side, believed the worst. In other words, he was a pessimist; he just couldn't believe things could possibly turn out right.

Sadly, in the history of our race, this fellow hasn't been the only one of his kind. The world has seen a few others. There has always been a contingent who have cried calamity and doom. Somebody writes:

My grandpa notes the world's worn cogs,
And says we're going to the dogs;
His granddad, in his house of logs,
Swore things were going to the dogs;
His dad, among the Flemish bogs,
Vowed things were going to the dogs;
The cave man, in his queer skin togs,
Said things were going to the dogs.
But this is what I wish to state;
The dogs have had an awful wait!

Recently a French scientist was asked what he saw on the human horizon to be optimistic about. He replied, "I am very optimistic about the future of pessimism." Well, of course, we've always had some of it; but it seems we have more of it now than we've ever had before. It has actually become popular to be pessimistic. I'm sure you remember the story of the shepherd boy who persistently alarmed everyone by crying "Wolf!" when no wolf was there. The "wolf cry" is heard often in our time. Again and again we are told that this or that wolf is scratching at the door, fangs bared to tear us apart. Many interpreters of the times, many of them "experts" more or less, have set up a noisy wail of doom: our human race is just about to be destroyed!

This theme is one of the most profitable areas of publication and journalism. We have a whole spate of articles and books, many of them big money makers, very convincingly telling us that anything and everything is about to happen: there'll be a chain reaction in the earth's atmosphere, or a depletion of the ozone layer, or a new ice age, or the insects will overcome us, or we'll run out of energy, or suffocate in our garbage, or poison ourselves with insecticides. It would seem we like to be scared; and it would seem there are many who like to scare us — and especially since scaring us is money in the bank for them. Pessimism is big business. And every new crier of doom is listened to like the voice of the Lord.

We have become victims of a horrible hypochondria; if I may coin a phrase, we are becoming psychological hypochondriacs. There is much pessimism concerning man. By many, man is seen as a nogoodnik (and that may be a new word, but if so, I think it's better than any other I can think of for use at this point). Too much we see ourselves as sick; and we don't see much hope. The tragic consequence is that it's terribly difficult to form a clear and affirmative image of tomorrow when we must look at it from within the psychological matrix of this popular pessimism.

Pessimism is defined as "an inclination to put the least favorable construction upon actions and happenings; to maximize adverse aspects, conditions, and possibilities; or to anticipate the worst possible outcome." That dictionary definition is an accurate description of an attitude which prevails in many segments of our modern life.

What kind of effect does all of this have? This distorted mentality — what are its consequences in our human life? First, it seems to me, it produces a form of creeping paralysis. A human who is afraid tends to be immobilized by his fear. One doesn't try very much if he doesn't belive in the outcome. He doesn't invest much in the future unless he can believe there is one.

This, it seems to me, is a tragic disservice we older people have perpetrated upon the younger people of our time: We have been so gloomy concerning humanity and the human future that we have almost taken the future away from them, and they are inclined to say, "What the heck — if the world is like this and the future is going to be like that, then what difference does it make what I think or how I act?" It is my conviction that whatever deviate and distressing patterns of attitude and conduct may exist among our younger people, they exist because of what we older people have done to their image of tomorrow. After all, for the young almost everything is in the future, somewhere; and if you take that away from them, there isn't much left. If the picture of the future is calamitous or uninviting, then it is almost inevitable that terrible inward devastation will occur. I have the uneasy feeling that many of the gloom-mongers of our time will have a lot to answer for.

Let's come to the point of all of this: Is there no alternative to all this gloom? I proclaim to you: There is. We need a friendly wind to drive the gloom away, a sunray to penetrate the pall, a light by which to exorcise this demon, a power to dispel all this despair. We need to find an antidote for the poison of all this pessimism.

I repeat the question: Is there no alternative to all this gloom? And I repeat the answer: There is. I speak with you out of the context of the Christian Faith, and I speak with you of hope. There isn't a pessimistic syllable in the entire New Testament record of the gospel of Christ, not one. Seen in right context, even the declarations of judgment are proclamations of hope — and especially these. Those writers lived in about the worst of times, but there isn't a gloomy word in all they said.

Yes, they realistically recognized the evils, dangers, and darkness around them, but all this they saw in context. They were able to view the bad news in the light of the good, the good news of Christ and change and hope. One of our problems in our time is that so many of us are unable to see our present in the light of anything bigger and brighter than it is. Unlike the doomsday exponents of our day, those New Testament writers were able to read the signs of their time under the rays of a brilliant light which beamed in from beyond it. For them the future was a primary reality, and the present was prelude.

You cannot thoughtfully read the New Testament writings of Paul and Peter and John without being struck by their firm conviction that tomorrow was a solution, not a problem; it was an answer, not a question. They were certain of it; eventually things would come right. Living by that image of tomorrow, they marched with triumph through the sufferings and problems and perils of their day. And as Christians, my dear friend, you and I must not permit the clouded issues of our time to eclipse that vision of tomorrow, for the vision is still valid; and whether or not we have comprehended this truth, for us of this Faith the future remains primary, and the present is prelude. Do you doubt this? I hope not. But if you do, I invite you to go again thoughtfully and prayerfully to your New Testament and read it for the answer to this one question: What was the meaning of the future for those people?

Whatever they saw in their time, they saw also that God was in it, touching it with redemption and hope. It has been often said that "pessimism is another name for atheism." True. You just cannot, with understanding, be a true theist and a pessimist at the same time. But when in every real and significant sense, God is pushed out of the picture, not much but gloom is left. A lot of people have made the mistake of leaving him out. O yes, they still name his name, and generally they would assert that they believe he is — somewhere, somehow, but not doing much of anything. But God isn't out; and he is not going to be; and he is not going to abandon his world or his people.

How much I wish each of us could have the eye-opening experience of Elisha's servant. Remember that story from 2 Kings, chapter six? The servant believed the armies of his people to be hopelessly surrounded by the overpowering hosts of the enemy. As he was wailing about the impending calamity, Elisha prayed, "Lord, open my servant's eyes." And the story is that his eyes were "opened," and round about them he saw that the mountains and valleys were filled with the horses and chariots of God! I know that this is picture language, but it is the picture of a profound truth, one we ought to recapture and never let go again. Also there was Elijah, intimidated by Jezebel, who ran into the woods and sat down in self-pity under a Juniper tree. But God said to him, "Get up and go," things are not all that bad. And he did — and they weren't.

In Hebrews 10:35 we Christians are told: *"Do not throw away your confidence."* I would like to emblazon those six words on the mind and spirit of every person who names the name of Christ. *Do not throw away your confidence.* It's your most priceless possession; keep it. Don't throw it away as though it didn't matter; it does.

I proclaim to you the power to purge this popular pessimism which is the scourge of our time — and it is the power of the gospel of Christ. The gospel was planned, designed, and arranged for this very world. I think the Planner knew what kind of world he was planning for, and I am quite sure the power he devoted to it is power sufficient. In our world have we reason for hope? Yes, I am confident we have many reasons; but had we no other, the Christian Faith is reason enough.

Take these insights, my friend; I offer them to you as a gift for your future. Take them; and of these materials build your image of tomorrow; and in the light of that image always see everything that stands this side of its fulfillment; and under the power and inspiration of it, move victoriously through all the days between now and then.

The Time of Our Visitation

Matthew 11:2-11
"Are you he who is to come . . .?"

You know how it was that Jesus of Nazareth began his career as a teacher and public figure in Galilee. You know how John came out of the wilderness and preached to the people who gathered around him on the banks of the Jordan. You know how for many long centuries the Jewish people had looked for the coming of their Messiah. When John appeared, their scholars speculated that perhaps this impassioned wilderness man might actually be the Expected One. They sent their representatives to inquire of him concerning this, saying, "Who are you?" And he said, "I am not the Christ" (John 1:19-20). Unsatisfied to know simply who John was *not*, they insisted on knowing who he *was:* "Who are you? What do you say about yourself?"

John never did really tell those people who he was. He identified himself only as a voice going before and preparing the way. Another was coming after him, he said, one mightier and more worthy; he it would be who would bring baptism with the Holy Spirit and with fire (Matthew 3:11-12). Now, if you heard somebody say something like that, wouldn't you look toward the horizon to see who would be coming next? Undoubtedly those people did, too. But John didn't let them wait long, for shortly, as Jesus came and stood in the company, John said, "There stands one among you whom you do not know" (John 1:26). And John cried out to all the people, "Behold! the Lamb of God, who takes away the sin of the world! This is he of whom I said, 'After me comes one who ranks before me, for he was before me.'" (John 1:30).

This is he! With these words the wilderness preacher identified Jesus, presented him to the people, and swung wide the doors upon the most spectacular three-year period in all of human history. Identities were very important there and then. Who was John? Who was Jesus? Those were important questions then. And, believe me, they are important questions now. Especially that one: Who was Jesus? A modern gospel song very movingly asks: "Do you know who Jesus is?" And one of our suppliant and hauntingly beautiful Negro spirituals confesses, "Lord, we didn't know who you was."

The identity of Jesus was apparently no question in the mind of John when he announced him to the world that day. But John was a preacher who preached against sin, and people usually don't like to have their sins preached against, and it would appear that this is especially true of kings. So King Herod had John arrested and thrown into prison. In the interval between his imprisonment and his execution, John apparently began to wonder about Jesus. I cannot tell you if his faith faltered or if he simply wanted reinforcement of it. Maybe the wonderful things he had foreseen weren't happening as quickly as he had expected them to. Anyway, sitting there in Herod's jail, John's heart hungered for a clear answer to the basic question: Who was Jesus?

So, as we read in Matthew 11, John sent messengers to Jesus with this question: "Are you he who is to come, or shall we look for another?" Let this be said for John: Even in jail, he was looking ahead, forward, hopefully turning to the future. He would look to Jesus, or if necessary, he would look beyond him; but as far as was necessary, he would look ahead. His question was: Would it be necessary to look farther than Jesus? One was to come — was Jesus he?

John's question is one of the most intriguing ever asked in any situation concerning anybody. But an even more intriguing aspect of this episode was the way Jesus answered the question, or the way, rather, he did not answer it. His reply was neither "yes" nor "no." When the messengers reached him, Jesus was busy with his ministering, giving sight to the blind, cleansing lepers, and proclaiming good news to the poor. And he simply said to the messengers, "Go and tell John what you hear and see." (Matthew 11:4). An oft-repeated theme of Jesus' was that a "tree is known by its fruits," (Matthew 7:20) and perhaps he was willing himself to stand under the judgment of that test, to leave it to harvest time to speak the answering word.

I strongly suspect, however, that Jesus had another reason for responding as he did. At least, ensuing events demonstrate that he might well have had. It is my feeling that he chose to give an answer that was nonverbal and not immediate. I think Jesus took John's question seriously, and I think he spent the next three years very consciously and conclusively answering it.

It's my purpose now to look with you into the record of subsequent events to see if we can find Jesus' answer to John's question. And may I say I am sure we can, and that the answer is a resounding "yes" with reverberating echoes that will never die away to the end of time and reach of eternity.

"Are you he who is to come?" John wished to know. Comings are important. A coming adds another dimension to almost any picture; it means change, whether it be the coming of a baby into a home, or the coming of Christ into the world, or the coming of the boss onto the job, or the coming of an armed robber to the door. Things happen when someone comes. A coming is the interjection of a new element, an additonal factor to be reckoned with. It may have no more significance than the dropping of a pebble into the ocean, or it may have all the significance of the San Francisco Earthquake.

The prospect that someone is coming into any situation or upon any scene instantly produces some interesting questions: Who is coming? When? Why? Where will the traveler meet us? And what will he do;

what impact will he have? There is a remarkable French drama by Samuel Becket entitled *Waiting for Goudot*. The entire plot is that two pathetic characters are waiting for someone to come. He is called Goudot. But who is Goudot, and why is he coming? We never know, because Goudot never comes. We are left with a whole complex of tantalizing questions as to the identity and mission of Goudot and what his coming might have meant had he come. The play doesn't say anything really; but it stands as something of a masterpiece, although it does nothing but explore the prospect of someone's coming.

Comings can be disappointing; they can promise more than they deliver; they can make a big splash, and when the waves are settled, it is seen that nothing much has happened. In a small Pennsylvania city about sixty years ago, a stranger showed up and rented a local theater for one night, the date being about a month hence. He bought space in the local newspaper and on every available billboard all around the town, and advertised intensively. The ads contained only three words — HE IS COMING! They didn't say who "he" was, why he was coming, or what he would do when he arrived. People bought tickets as they had never bought tickets before, and when came the appointed evening, the theater was filled as nobody had ever seen it filled. When came the appointed hour, the house lights dimmed, the curtain went up, the stage lights came on, and the audience saw on the stage simply a huge banner reading: HE IS GONE! And, of course, the promoter also was gone — with all the money from the greatest ticket sale anybody had ever heard of. And the people, looking at one another in stunned amazement, said, "We've been had." And, indeed, they had been had.

Well, John had said concerning Jesus, "This is he," and he had believed that. Now he wanted to know if Jesus would turn out to be a disappointment to him, and if he would have to look beyond him for the coming of another. And Jesus, it would appear, answered John's question by simply saying: Let events speak for themselves. So, here and now, my good friend, let us let the events speak, and let us listen carefully to what the events are saying.

First, we look in upon one which occurred after almost three years had gone by. As you and I look back upon it from here, it was nearly two thousand years ago on the Sunday before that first Easter Sunday. Jerusalem was teeming with the multitudes who were keeping the Passover. And Jesus came! This is the Palm Sunday scene. Jesus came, riding on a borrowed burro, riding into the city of Jerusalem, and the record paints the scene this way: "As Jesus was drawing near, at the descent of the mount of Olives, the whole multitude of the disciples began to rejoice and praise God with a loud voice for all the mighty works that they had seen" (Luke 19:37). By this time they had seen many. But their mood of exuberant praise was one the Pharisees did not share, and they said to Jesus, "Teacher, rebuke your disciples." Perhaps the long-faced, phylactery-wearing Pharisees felt Jesus' disciples were making too much noise. Jesus, apparently, did not share this feeling, for his reply was this: "I tell you, if these were silent, the very stones would cry out." Then as the procession drew near and Jesus saw the city, he wept over it, saying: "The days shall come upon you when your enemies shall cast a bank about you, and hem you in on every side, and dash you to the ground — you and your children within you — and they shall not leave one stone upon another — because *you did not know the time of your visitation.*" (Luke 19:41-44).

There he was, there at the gate of the city, and they did not know that this was he. Yes, they knew that his name was Jesus; but they didn't comprehend who Jesus was. They knew the *name* of the Man; but they did not know the *Man.* And those Palm Sunday Pharisees and multitudes were members of a large company of others who have been likewise unaware.

John's Gospel tells us that Jesus came into our world and "the world knew him not" (John 1:10). He came to Bethlehem and angels sang, and a few people heard and saw — but most never knew he was there. He came to Nazareth and there lived and worked and walked the village streets — but most never knew that it was he. They could call him by name and say, "Good morning, Jesus," when they passed him in the way; but they believed they were speaking to the apprentice who was learning the carpenter's trade down at Joseph's village shop. And at length Jesus came to Calvary and to the cross, and it was Good Friday. To most who saw him there, he died as a common criminal, and they didn't understand. To most of the people to whom Jesus came — wherever and whenever — he was, tragically, "The Unidentified One." How appropriate, then, is the word of Jesus spoken at Jerusalem's city gate that first Palm Sunday morning: "You did not know the time of your visitation." And it could equally well be said of Bethlehem and Nazareth and most of the rest of the world.

It seems we human beings have trouble knowing what time it is, identifying the hour. So frequently we do not grasp the magnitude of a moment until sometime after. Christopher Morley has this interesting line: "Never write up your diary on the day itself; it takes longer than that to know what happened!" In our personal lives, and in the great sweeps of history, we so often fail to see the golden hour in its own time — only later, looking back. It seems we almost never know the time of our visitation.

So often we are visited by opportunity, only to pass it by with averted gaze, and later, looking back, say, "I wish I had . . ." So often we are visited by high privilege, but being so preoccupied with some trivia or so busy complaining about something or other, we let the privilege pass, and only in some more reflective aftertime do we realize what treasure we trifled away.

Lowell wrote, "Once to every man and nation comes the moment to decide." But with what frequency that moment goes by in default because as it came and went, we were looking some other way. Shakespeare put it this way: "There is a tide in the affairs of men, which taken at the flood, leads on to fortune." But somehow we of humankind have a strange proclivity for missing the tide; while it flows in and out, we debate and hesitate as to the most propitious time of launching, and when it's all gone we are still right where we were.

Often we are like Jacob at Bethel, who, after that strange heaven-visited night, said, "Surely God was in this place and I did not know it" (Genesis 28:16). Often we are like those two men who walked the road from Jerusalem to Emmaus, and Jesus drew near and walked with them, and afterward it was said that they did not know it was Jesus. And being like this, we can miss so much.

The story is told of a young couple who had just brought their newborn baby home from the hospital. They were exposed to all the meaning and wonder and miracle of their own firstborn child. The dewey-eyed young mother came upon her husband standing beside the child's crib very reflectively looking down into it. Quietly she approached him, slipped her arm around his, and said, "A penny for your thoughts, darling." He was silent for another moment, and then shook his head and said, "I was just trying to figure out how in the world they can sell a crib like that for ten dollars and ninety-nine cents!"

Being like that, we can miss so much. I am reminded of a cartoon picturing an American home scene. The setting is in the living room, and the lady has a guest with whom she is talking. Present in the other end of the room is the lady's husband, in his undershirt, his feet on a table, a drinking glass in one hand, a couple of day's growth of whiskers on his face, newspaper sports sections scattered about, a transistor radio firmly held to his ear, intently watching a football game on television. And the lady is saying to her guest, "I *did* leave him once, but he never noticed!"

Well, Jesus was saddened and grieved that Jerusalem was missing so much — because they did not know the time of their visitation. But I am not speaking here about what *they* were missing. I am not thinking here about the time of *their* visitation. I am thinking and speaking about the time of *our* visitation and about what *we* might be missing.

You ask: When is the time of our visitation? I wish all questions were as easily answered as this one. The answer is: *now.* Right now — whatever year it is, whatever month, or week, or day of the week, or hour of the day — right now. The question has been sometimes raised: Do we on earth have visitors from outer space? May there possibly be non-humans from elsewhere walking our streets, moving in our midst? I don't know. There may be; there may not be. I don't know about strangers on our streets. But I do know this: God has sent his Son to this world, and he is here, and he says, "I am with you" (Matthew 28:20). He says, "The Father has sent me" (John, chapters 5 through 17). He says, "I came from the Father" (John 16:28). It was the late J. B. Phillips who declared: "Ours is a *visited* planet." I would like to echo that declaration. As an African tom-tom drummer picks up a distant sound, and beats it out, and sends the message on, I would like to relay this revelation to the ends of the earth: ours is a visited planet.

And the Visitor will not go away; he will not abandon us; he will not leave us alone. He has invested himself totally in us, even unto death; he has identified himself completely with us, even to taking our own sins upon himself; he has entered into all we can ever feel, and no need of ours is ever beyond his skill. He has come to this world and bought it with his blood, laid claim to it by his love; and he is not going to surrender his world to the greedy, or the mighty, or the power-mad, or the vain, or to any sensual and licentious animal. With compassionate eyes he is pleading; with wounded hands he is beckoning; and he calls us to our knees, and from our knees to our feet, and from the paths of earth at last to the golden streets of glory.

At Bethlehem he came to our world — and most people didn't know it. At Calvary he came to our hearts — and many of us don't know it. At the Easter dawn he came forth to stand forever before the world — and there he stands — and he speaks to your heart and mine, and he says, "Behold! I stand at the door and knock" (Revelation 3:20). That's present tense; I am standing, I am knocking. He who came long ago comes now. It wasn't just yesterday, that we should find him only as a record and a memory. It isn't just tomorrow, that we should know him only as a hope. But it's now. This is the time of our visitation.

A little while ago, writing in *The Upper Room*, a lady named Hazel Hughes told a story which has meant much to me. While a student, she had as her botany teacher a wonderful, kindly, elderly gentleman. She wrote that one day during his lecture she must have mentally wandered away, for later she could remember nothing that he had said. But suddenly, as he spoke, she was aware that his soft voice was patiently and compassionately directed to her personally, for she heard him saying, "Hazel Hughes, I have looked at you all morning, and you have not looked at me once." The thought that her inattention had disappointed and offended this good man struck her with shame. And when I read that school-days story, I thought how many times my Lord Christ may have occasion to say to me, "Leonard Mann, I have been looking at you all morning, and you haven't looked at me once." All morning? Yes, perhaps, and maybe longer. Maybe, for some, an entire lifetime.

Christ comes to you and me with the gift of forgiveness and peace and freedom and hope and salvation and life. And he is knocking at our door and waiting for us to open it. He is looking at us, and waiting for us to turn and look at him. The time of our visitation is now.

Look thoughtfully and reverently at the career of Jesus on planet Earth, and you will see a dramatic confirmation of this. We have here a drama in three acts; and the first is that birth at Bethlehem. It was attended by certain uncommon circumstances; there were those who said the stars did unusual things and that heavenly voices were heard from the skies. But whatever the physical phenomena surrounding his birth, we know that his coming to the world did indeed make an impact, did get attention and stir things up. This was true at the time of his birth and also later.

People knew Jesus was around! To know where he was, just follow the crowds! And he had a word for everybody. If they were arrogant purveyors and paraders of their own virtue, they heard him say, "You are whitewashed tombs filled with dead men's bones" (Matthew 23:27). If they were repentant seekers and hungry of heart, they heard him say, "Your sins are forgiven you" (Luke 7:48). He lived about thirty-three years, and some may say that that was that. But not quite — not in the case of Jesus. He didn't quit when he was thirty-three. There was something about him that Pontius Pilate could not stop, something that neither the Jerusalem hierarchy nor the Roman Empire could bring to an end. And this brings us to the second act in the drama: his death.

Most people, born into the world, manage to get themselves identified somewhat with the humanity which inhabits this globe. They come onto the scene and move to some extent into it. Some may go no farther than to be merely identified with a family. Others may achieve identification in some way with a community. And a few will reach into history.

Observe how this happens. Beethoven worked hard, struggled, suffered, and strove — and got himself identified with a portion of humankind as a maker of music to inspire and lift the spirits of men. Lincoln worked hard, struggled, suffered, and strove — and got himself identified with a segment of humankind as a champion of liberty and of the dignity and worth of human life. John Doe worked hard, struggled, suffered, and strove — and got himself identified with a part of humankind as a bricklayer who had the skill to help his fellowmen to put down their pavements and build their houses.

But Jesus went farther. In identifying with humankind, Jesus went farther than anybody else has ever gone. Many people have done wonderful things with their lives, and so did Jesus. But he also did something with his death, something nobody else has ever done. He didn't give just the skills of the musician or the statesman or the craftsman. By means of death, he gave his life. He used death as an instrument of conveyance.

Others have made their partial identifications with humankind for this or that service on this or that level; but Jesus made a total identification with all of humankind in the full dimension of all our sufferings, sorrows, burdens, troubles, and sins. He got to us, involved himself with us, as nobody else ever has. What happened at Bethlehem brought him to the world; what happened at Calvary brought him to the threshold of every human life; and this was the second act in the mighty drama of his coming.

But we have not gotten the message of the drama in its fullness until we have viewed act three. The scene is set in the garden where is located the new tomb which belongs to Joseph of Arimathea, the tomb in which no body has ever been laid — not until last Friday evening when the disciples of Jesus had removed the body of Jesus from the cross and brought it here. Now, on Sunday morning, a huge stone bars the entry-way, the security seal of the Roman Empire is on it, and armed soldiers stand guard nearby. And here this morning something happens. And afterward we hear Jesus saying, "I am he who lives and was dead, and, behold, I am alive forevermore" (Revelation 1:18 K.J.V.).

Forevermore! It is of much interest that they who had killed him never tried to do it again. Forevermore! He who at Calvary had gotten himself all the way to the threshold of every human life has now on his resurrection day established himself in that position forever.

You see, his coming was very very successfully accomplished. It was complete. He came all the way. He didn't quit where most servants of humanity must. They do their best, and then they say goodby, and death comes and takes them away. But not Jesus; he says, "I will see you again," (John 16:22) and death comes, but it doesn't take him away; it brings him closer than he was before, and he says, "I am with you."

For all the rest of us, death is the instance of our going, but for Jesus it was an aspect of his coming. By means of it, he comes nearer to us; and by the miracle of his resurrection, he stands there forever.

Yes, the time of our visitation is now. And John's inquiry of Jesus — "Are you he who is to come, or shall we look for another?" — has been answered now. And he has answered it for all time. And his answer is not in word only, but is in power, and in his living presence.

There is an ancient legend that Bethlehem's innkeeper stood with others at Mount Calvary that Friday when Jesus died. The legend has the innkeeper saying something like this: "When he came to my inn many years ago, I did not let him in because I did not know who he was, and I did not know that he was coming, and I wasn't looking for him when he came. And now, having seen him die, I do not think he is dead. I have the feeling that he could come at any time and knock on any door."

It seems to me that Jesus has given quite a satisfactory answer to John's ancient question. And I think history has confirmed it. After all, we have had almost two thousand years to improve upon Christ, and we haven't done it. He still stands as the hinge of history. Time is still dated from his birth. And all the evidence is declaring, "Yes, John, he who is to come *is come*." Not just has come, but is. He came not just to an ancient time, but to all time, not just to an ancient people, but to all people. His destination was not Bethlehem or Mount Calvary or the Resurrection Garden; these were but milestones he passed on the journey. His real destination is our own individual inner spirits, the objective of his coming to reach the depths of our hearts and minds, to find spiritual admission into our inward selves, to take repossession of the spirit which the Creator in his own image implanted there, and in peace and power to occupy what the heavenly Father claims as his own.

So he comes all the way; and having come, he is always coming, with each new appearance as immediate as the next opening of a door; for he says, "Behold, I am standing at the door, and I am knocking." And this has been true ever since that first Easter morning. Please notice something which happened that very evening. John 20:19: "Then that same day at evening, when the doors were shut where the disciples were assembled for fear of the Jews, came Jesus, and stood in the midst of them, and said, Peace be unto you."

Jesus had now been three days crucified, and his disciples were gravely afraid of the same powers that had crucified him. They were huddled in a secret place, and the doors were shut. But there was a rumor amongst them, a glimmer of hope: Peter and John had been to the tomb, and had discovered that the body of Jesus was not there. Two women of their number had reported that Jesus was alive, that they had seen him, that he had spoken to them. Could this possibly be true? And if it were true, what would be the meaning of it?

Then came Jesus. This is what the record says. Then came Jesus. At that very moment! to those very people! in that very place! in all their fear, bewilderment, uncertainty, and need! Then came Jesus. He came to them — and he couldn't have come at a better time; they never needed him more. Yes, I suppose, when Jesus arose, he might have gone straightway back to heaven and sat down at the Father's side in glory; but he didn't. He sought out that little, huddled company of confused and troubled disciples. It was almost as though he had walked forth from the grave with the specific purpose of meeting his friends again, and of letting them know for sure that everything was all right. It was their moment of deepest despair and anxiety, but then came Jesus.

There were also other times he came. There was Mary Magdalene, sin-stained, whom he had touched and transformed; and she stood beside the vacated tomb, like a lost child, not understanding, and alone — but then came Jesus, not from within the tomb, but from outside it, and he said, "Mary!" and she knew him, and she ran — not weeping, but rejoicing — to tell the others that she had seen the Lord, alive.

Two or three years afterward, Saul of Tarsus was on the road from Jerusalem to Damascus, carrying warrants for the arrest of the Christians there, hatred seething within him, but then came Jesus, accosting Saul on the road beneath the noonday sun; and the man Saul was never the same again. The voice that once had "breathed threatenings and slaughter against the disciples of the Lord" (Acts 9:1) became the most significant voice of Christian witness this world has ever heard.

About half a century later an aged Christian named John was imprisoned on the Island of Patmos in the Aegean Sea. Because of his faith, this man had been stripped of his possessions and rights of citizenship. Alone, cut off and shut away from the rest of the world, this patriarch of the Faith had every reason to despair.

But then came Jesus, and John said, "He laid his right hand on me, and he said to me: Write" (Revelation 1:16-19). And John wrote — the incomparable vision of victory which stands now as the final book of the Christian Bible, and one of the most hopeful and courage-engendering things ever to come from the pen of any man.

But the comings of Jesus did not cease when the New Testament book of history closed. He has done a lot of coming this side of that. If you could ask John Wesley concerning the dramatic transformation of his life, I think you would hear him say, "I was defeated and frustrated and lost; all my doings were mechanical, the making of motions, with no spirit and no joy; that's the way it was with me — but then came Jesus, and I found my heart was strangely warmed within me." And, of course, you can multiply the witness of Wesley a great many millions of times and write it over the signatures of some of the world's greatest leaders and servants of men.

Aren't you glad, my friend, that you and I are living on the post-Easter side of history? — that in our time any story of human quest and struggle might well somewhere include these three turn-around words, then came Jesus? A little while ago there was on American television an interesting dramatic series entitled *And Then Came Bronson*. The plot of each story was about the same as all the others: there was some kind of crisis situation, a time of desperate need, and just then young Bronson would ride in from nowhere on his motorcycle, untangle all the mess, see that justice was done, and then ride away into the sunset, into the mystery out of which he came. Well, all that Bronson could ever do is as nothing compared with what Christ so often does and always can.

Here, on this side of his having died, the living Christ comes to us offering not only comfort for our dying, but wings for our living — here and now, tomorrow and always. To say "Then came Jesus" is to tell only a part of the story, the past part. To tell the rest of it, put it into the present tense: *Now* Comes Jesus. You may be lonely, troubled, perplexed, laden with the guilt of sin, shackled to a bad past, shut in or shut out, but now comes Jesus, offering to you forgiveness for all the clouded yesterdays and hope and power and a guiding hand for new tomorrows.

No, I do not understand all the miracles of his coming. I do not understand many aspects of his infant-coming at Bethlehem; but he came, and things happened because he did. I do not understand his coming to that place called Calvary; but he came, and things happened because he did. I do not understand his coming forth from Joseph's tomb, breaking the seal of Rome and the bonds of death; but he did, and things happened because he did. I do not understand his coming to a human person trapped in the quagmires, lost in the wilderness, pursued by the hounds of fear; but he comes, and things happen because he does. But I don't have to understand; the miracle of his redeeming love is its own witness, and this is enough.

We say we believe in God — at least most of us do. And if we do, then let us understand that the entire personal power of this God in whom we believe, insofar as it can possibly relate to us as human creatures, has been incarnated in Jesus Christ, and set down in our midst. This is the gospel. This is the good news. And, comprehending this, one does not continue to go about "business as usual."

In the upper room of that Jerusalem home that Thursday night of Jesus' last earthly week he said a momentous thing which we often miss in our casual reading. It's in John, chapter 14. Jesus said to his apostles, "You believe in God . . . believe also in me." He is saying you do believe in God; now I ask you to believe also in me. You do believe that God is; now I ask you to believe also that he has expressed himself. You do believe in the God who is out there somewhere; now I ask you believe also that in me he has come in very close to you. You do believe that God loves and cares; now I ask you to believe also that he is acting as if he does.

Yes, John, you yonder in Herod's prison, rejoice and be at peace. We don't altogether understand how it is that he comes to us when we need him so much — in the dark night of our trouble or sorrow, in the long day of our toil, in the fierce crucible of any storm that may swirl around us, but he comes, and he is saying, "Take heart; it is I; do not be afraid" (Matthew 14:27).

Yes, John, you were right about the Man, right in what you first said. Perhaps you didn't understand everything either, and perhaps the question arose in your mind as in your prison cell you pondered the mystery of him. But it was the right question, John; and, in answering it for you, he has answered it for us, and his answer is this: Yes, I am he who is to come, and you need not look for any other.

A Faith for the Uncharted Way

Matthew 1:18-25
"He did as the angel of the Lord commanded him . . ."

A few summers ago my family and I made a motor trip west from our home in Ohio to the Pacific coast, and returned. We crossed the prairies and the plains, the Mojave Desert and the great salt flats of Utah; we drove through the Badlands and the Grand Tetons, and crossed the Sierra Nevadas and the Rocky Mountains twice. We followed the trails of the pioneers, the Mojave, the Wyoming, and the Santa Fe. We traveled on good roads in a good automobile with a good road map. We had never been in any of that country before, but we were never lost once, nor did we ever miss the road and have to turn around and go back.

As we traveled, though, I kept remembering others who had traveled there before us, pilgrims and pioneers who had ventured into a land that was then unknown. I thought of their struggles to locate the river crossings and find the mountain passes, their confrontation with the unknown which always lay just around the next bend of the river or beyond the next hilltop. We had our road map to guide us and to alert us to what lay ahead; but they had neither road map nor road. They always stood at the edge of the unknown, at the borderline of the unexplored.

And I thought of life, our life, yours and mine. Like pilgrims and pioneers, we, too, always are standing at the edge of the unknown. No scout has gone into the future and returned to tell us what is out there. We must move into it not knowing. It hasn't been charted yet; nobody has been there to photograph it and bring back the picture. And if we are going ahead — and we must — we need a faith for the uncharted way.

Looking back over the road we have chosen, we can see somewhat clearly; but as we turn the other way, from whatever vantage point we look, there is nothing that we can see. Yes, we can form our images and paint our pictures, and we must; but tomorrow is not yet unveiled and cannot be until time pulls aside the curtain and lets us see. It is very true that we "do not know what a day may bring forth" (Proverbs 27:1). We are living constantly in a continuous encounter with the unknown.

A small girl, at the beginning of her learning process, said, "Momma, do I *know* as much as I *don't* know?" I doubt if any of us does. Whatever the number of days we may have mastered and logged, tomorrow is still a mystery, its unexplored expanse as yet unmapped; and when we enter it — and enter it we must — we must go by faith, the faith of the pilgrim and the pioneer. The road that is as yet untraveled is always an unanswered question, and sometimes it may appear to loom as an insoluble problem.

Have you ever considered what surely must have been the terrible trauma of Joseph of Nazareth when he first learned about Mary and the Baby? You know he was engaged to be married to Mary. And I think Joseph was a good man, hard-working, honest, gentle, kind, and clean. How intense must have been the pain within him upon learning that a baby was growing in her womb — the reverent and beautiful Mary, pregnant! This quiet and respected young woman of their village, soon to bear a child! Something, it must have appeared to Joseph, was terribly wrong. His pastoral and placid image of tomorrow must suddenly have been struck by storm.

Now I suppose Joseph was an ordinary carpenter-type of man, good with tools and at shaping and smoothing wood. But I doubt if he was well-read in philosophy or if his mind was at ease wrestling with the vast imponderables of life and time and space and God. What then must have been the awesome impact of the vision which came to him in a dream that night. You know about that dream, don't you? You know, as Joseph slept, an angel appeared to him and said to him, "Joseph, son of David, do not fear to take Mary your wife, for that which is conceived in her is of the Holy Spirit; she will bear a son, and you shall call his name Jesus, for he will save his people from their sins" (Matthew 1:20-21).

Think, my friend, of awakening from a dream like that! Think of the thousand intermingled questions and hopes and fears which must have immediately tumbled over one another in the humble carpenter's mind and spirit. Into his plans for the future had suddenly been interjected vast and unprecedented elements of mystery, with dimensions of meaning and impact far beyond his power to understand or even guess.

But what did the carpenter do? He did precisely what the angel said he should. He took Mary as his wife, waited for the Child to be born, and when he was, he named him Jesus. Joseph didn't panic in the presence of the unknown; he moved into the future as though he believed in it.

Well, you and I, struggling with the problems of the day and the unanswered questions concerning tomorrow, do not always have an angel to come and tell us what's happening and what we ought to do. We have to move into the future without the benefit of angels — at least the kind of angels that visit us in our dreams and show us which way to go. Yes, perhaps we have our angels that speak in other forms and other ways, and I'm sure we do. But, whatever the source and mode of the guidance we get, we have to move into the future by faith, the faith of the pilgrim and the pioneer, the faith of one who walks where no one has ever walked before, the faith that is for the uncharted way. And for this kind of going on, I recommend the Christian Faith.

No, the Christian Faith is not the answer to all the quesions of the universe. It does, however, offer an answer which renders most of the questions unnecessary. The Christian Faith is not a solution to all the mysteries of life; but it does provide a solution in the light of which the mysteries are no longer seen as enemies, but as our friends and allies. This Faith is not an automatic answer to every question, but is rather a way of making the questions tolerable and meaningful and helpful. In a child's arithmetic book, the answers may be printed in the back. The book of life is not equipped with answers provided in such a way. At no point as we peruse the pages can we turn to the back of the book and look the answers up. We live the book of life page by page, and wait.

Here, however, is what the Christian Faith does: It lets us know that if we add two and two correctly, we will get the right answer. It lets us know that if we work through the problems by the rules, we won't need to worry about what the answer page will say. And, of course, this Faith lets us know that if we don't put it together rightly, we'll be judged by what we find when we turn the last page. In other words, this Faith fixes it so we don't have to know all the answers now; the end is not yet; all we have to know is the way, and we can trust the end. This Faith is assuring us that if we can hear Jesus as he says, "I am the way," and take him as the way, and know that he has overcome, we'll not ever have to worry about the outcome. It is this insight of faith which prompted one of our poets to give us these lines:

So I go on not knowing;
I would not if I might;
I would rather walk in the dark with God
Than to walk alone in the light;
I would rather walk with him by faith
Than to walk alone by sight.

It is undoubtedly this aspect of faith which inspired the writing of this oft-quoted sentiment for the New Year: "I said to the man who stood at the gate of the year, 'Give me a sight that I might tread safely into the unknown.' And he said to me, 'Go out and put your hand into the hand of God, and that shall be unto thee better than sight and safer than a known way.' "

It is this assurance quality of faith which makes it the springboard of courage and everlasting venture. As people of faith, we'll never be defeated or made to despair by what we do not know. Whittier wrote:

When on my day of life the night is falling,
And in the wind from unsunned spaces blown,
I hear far voices out of darkness calling
My feet to paths unknown . . .

Of course, the poet is writing of the great adventure called death. But there are also other adventures this side of death, and to these also we can sometimes hear "far voices" calling. Winds from unilluminated areas bring to us voices that say: Come on, come on into tomorrow. Sometimes these voices arise from areas of human need, dismal and unsunned spaces in the human scene — spaces that may be geographical or spiritual or moral or intellectual. And we are called to move on out, and go.

Do you remember the story of Robert Moffatt, the British missionary who first explored the inner dark of Africa? Fired with a passion to get the Christian gospel into that continent, Moffatt returned to England and said, "I have stood on a mountain top in Africa and have seen the smoke of a thousand villages where no white man has ever been." David Livingstone heard Moffatt say that, and Livingstone went, and his going is another story. He heard the far voices calling, and he plunged into the African jungles more deeply than anyone before him had ever dared. During Livingstone's many years there, some well-meaning people in England offered to send others to help him, if, they said, "there is a good road to get to where you are." Livingstone's famous reply was, "If they you propose to send must have a good road to get here, then I cannot use them."

Well, the far voices are calling us — and always to paths unknown. For a time I was in theology classes taught by Professor Frank Paul Morris. (As I mention his name, I wish to pay tribute to a good and great-hearted man — and somewhat of an eccentric, too. How well I remember him as the teacher who always carried his books in a basket.) Dr. Morris had a unique way of looking over his glasses at us students and saying, "Young men, you don't know what you are preparing for. You may think you know, but you don't. You are actually preparing for the day when your great test will come. Prepare well." He was right; it is true; we never really know what we are preparing for — except that it is to walk in paths unknown.

The far voice of time is calling us on. Changes will come. For time to stand still would stop experience; the passing of time is the one prerequisite for anything happening. The far voice of age also is calling us on. It is the inevitable by-product of our having lived long enough to reach it. And it is a reward or a penalty as we let it be. The far voice of pain is another which is forever calling us on. Inescapable, it calls out of the darkness yonder, and says come on and meet me here. But there are other far voices, too — voices such as the voice of glory and of joy and of home. And they call us out, and on, and up. And the most wonderful of the far voices calling is the voice heard by the Apostle Paul and described to us as "the upward call of God in Christ Jesus" (Philippians 3:14).

As we stand at the edge of the unknown, let us hear the far voices, and not ever fear them. We cannot tell what word of summons they will bear, but we can be ready for them when they come. Robert Louis Stevenson, author of *Treasure Island* and many other fine adventure stories, a devout and sincere Christian, was a victim of tuberculosis and spent many years suffering the weakness and pain of the disease. His step-daughter, Isobel Field, in *This Life I've Loved*, wrote the following: "One day Stevenson read us a prayer he had just written. In it were words none of us will ever forget: 'When the day returns, call us up with morning faces and morning hearts, eager to labor, happy if happiness be our portion, and if the day be marked for sorrow, strong to endure.' We awakened on the morrow with happy morning faces ... (But) that day was marked for sorrow. That day, at the height of his fame, in the best of health he had ever enjoyed, Louis went out of this life suddenly, quietly, painlessly."

Yes, the far voices are forever calling, and life's finest adventures are in gracefully and heartily answering their call, day by day, page by page, as the leaves are turned. Most people admire Christopher Columbus, his courage and venture. We admire him not because he sat by the seaside with his chin in his hand; we admire him because he unfurled the sails of three small ships and pointed them toward the unknown west. On that voyage to the new world, across waters where no man had ever been, there were no charted islands to say they had passed, no landfalls to enter on the log, no odometer to tell them how far they had gone, no map to suggest how far they would have to go; and so each day in the logbook Columbus wrote one simple line: This day we sailed on.

And this is life: we know where we are only in relation to where we have been, and we never know how far it is to what. But we don't have to know. If we make our voyage with this Faith as our guide, let our logbook show that "This day we sailed on" and that every sunset finds us looking forward to another dawn.

Speaking of logbooks, there was the intrepid explorer Fridtjof Nansen and his voyage to the North Pole. At one point in the ship's log, Nansen made this entry: "We let down thirty-five hundred fathoms and touched no bottom." In our voyage of life, sailing through strange waters, we don't know how deep they are either. But we don't have to know, for the depth of the water doesn't matter when you're on top of it. Mystery? If we are living by faith, we can live with that.

Albert Einstein said, "The most beautiful thing we can experience is a sense of the mysterious; it is the source of all art and all science." And may I add: it is also the congenial traveling companion of all faith. For faith can take mystery's hand and agreeably walk with her on any journey he makes.

And faith can also walk with danger. Herein is one of faith's great values — for there is a lot of danger. Some people walk this trail and some that. There are divergent ways, and some are purposeful and some are pointless. On the rear bumper of an automobile I saw a sticker with this message: "Don't follow me; I'm lost." Being lost is not a condition to be proud of, but no doubt a lot of people are lost. There are paths that criss-cross and intersect and wind and twist this way and that. There are broad ways and narrow, high ways and low, mountain trails and valley roads. There are trails that are crooked and highways that are straight, and some lead here and some yonder; some climb and some descend; some go somewhere and some just go round and round. Some trails are crowded and the travelers nudge and shove one another along the way, and others are lonely. But all are trails; and some people walk this one and some walk that — but there is one trail that everybody walks, and it is the trail of uncertainty, insecurity, and peril.

Playwright Thornton Wilder gives us this line: "We walk on a thin edge of danger." The Old Testament psalmist was aware of this: "I am a stranger and a sojourner as all my fathers were" (Psalms 39:12); "My soul is continually in my hand" (Psalms 119:109); "I walk in the midst of trouble" (Psalms 138:7); "My soul is among lions" (Psalms 57:4). Most of us know this, and we know it well. We know something of what is meant in Amos 5:19 where it is said that it is "as if a man fled from a lion, and a bear met him; or went into the house and leaned his hand against the wall, and a serpent bit him." Wilder was right; we do indeed walk on a thin edge of danger.

This fact is most apparent to most of us; sooner or later we can assemble many personal illustrations of the truth of it. Job, in the midst of his grave afflictions, went so far as to say at one point: "Man is born to trouble as the sparks fly upward" (Job 5:7). I know it seems sometimes that almost nothing works out right, that we are hounded by a kind of malevolency. I read of a minor playwright in New York who felt this way about things. Having been plagued by a series of what he considered misfortunes, he wrote a little fantasy in which he cast himself as the central figure. One morning, as God looked down on the earth, he said to Gabriel, "What's that fellow doing down there?" And Gabriel said, "He's relaxing in his front yard smelling a flower." And God said, "So he is, is he? Well, send down a bee to sting him." That little fantasy is intended to be humorous as I am using it here, and of course it is an overdrawing of the picture, because God just doesn't work that way.

But the fact remains: we do walk on a thin edge of danger. You've often heard recitals of "famous last words." Some such words: "I'll light a match to see if there's gas in the tank," or "That sign says the bridge is out, but I don't believe it," or "I think I'll see how fast it will run." I want to add another one: "I'm all set." I'm all fixed; I have things arranged just the way I want them. Well, things have a way of not staying put. There is this about our life situations: things change. Comfort, and then sudden pain. As is suggested in 1 Thessalonians 5:3, "When people say, 'There is peace and security' then sudden destruction will come."

We can tuck life's components neatly into pigeonholes, and the next time we look, it is as though a tornado has struck. We can spread our picnic beneath the sun, but it can rain. We can sing "Don't let it rain on my parade," but it will — sooner or later. The most sophisticated Fifth Ave parlor dog will occasionally have to scratch a flea. And fleas have their problems, too. At least Jonathan Swift thought so as he wrote:

> So naturalists observe, a flea
> Hath smaller fleas that on him prey,
> And these have smaller ones to bite 'em,
> And so proceed ad infinitum.

We may arise in the morning singing, "O what a beautiful morning, O what a beautiful day; everything's going my way," and by evening we may be saying with Sara Teasdale:

My soul is a dark plowed field in the cold rain;
My soul is a broken field plowed by pain.

Yes, we walk on a thin edge of danger; and we need a faith for walking here. I'm trying to say to you that in the Christian Faith we have it. The Old Testament psalmist knew about trouble and he knew about God. It strikes me, as I read the psalms, that the psalmist was expert in two areas: trouble and God. He knew more about both than most people ever learn; and he was a master at relating the one with the other. In Psalms 22:11 he prays, "Be not far from me, for trouble is near." As he saw it, a reason for God's nearness was trouble's presence. In Psalm 91 he cites God's attitude toward the human sufferer: "I will be with him in trouble."

My mother (if I may speak personally for a moment) knew many pains and heartaches in the short forty-five years of her lifetime. I can remember how she used to sing as she went about her household chores at our farm home. As a small lad, I heard the words:

He walks with me, and he talks with me,
And he tells me I am his own;
And the joy we share, as we tarry there,
None other has ever known.

I did not then understand the meaning of those words. I supposed the song was a romantic ballad of some sort. Who "he" was I didn't know; but in my child's mind I sensed he was someone very special. It took me several years to learn that my mother, out of her sufferings and trials, was singing of the presence of her Lord. Yes, indeed, my friend, we have a Faith for this walk — along the thin edge of any danger.

There's a lot of talk in our time about security. It's a kind of mania with us, almost. We want to be relieved of all risk. We are concerned about economic security, social security, job security, military security, psychological security. We plan and devise, and make security our aim. But what kind of security is there, if any? With death certain, any security worthy of the name must be a kind which surpasses it. With pain imminent, it must be a kind that can transcend the physical, embrace it, use it, and survive it.

I think there is indeed such a security. It is not one which shields us from all hurt. Rather it is one which takes us beyond it and connects us with eventuations. It is the security of knowing that ultimately the spiritual outlives the physical, that at length joy overcomes sorrow, that life survives death. It is the kind of security John Wesley must have had when a lady asked him, "Supposing that you knew you were to die at twelve o'clock tomorrow night — how would you spend the intervening time?" Wesley's famous answer was: "How, madam? Why, just as I intend to spend it now. I should preach this evening at Gloucester, and again at five tomorrow morning; after that I should ride to Tewkesbury, preach in the afternoon and meet the society in the evening; I should then repair to friend Martin's house, who expects to entertain me, converse and pray with the family as usual; retire at ten o'clock, commend myself to my heavenly Father; lie down to rest and wake up in glory."

This is the kind of security Ignatius of Loyola must have had when, as a student, he was playing in a ball game with his fellow-students, and someone suddenly and solemnly demanded to know what each student would do if he knew he must die within twenty minutes. All agreed they would rush to the chapel and pray — all but Ignatius, that is; and he said, "I would finish the game."

This is the only kind of security I know of — the security of the ready. It is the security of the poised, those who belong to God, who are at home and at peace with life, who can see beyond the immediate and know that all is well. Deep in a coal mine a visitor asked the men how they could endure working under such oppressive and dangerous conditions. One miner answered, "We live close to dynamite and close to God." We all live close to dynamite; but if we also live close to God, we are not put into panic by the proximity of the dynamite. I am trying to say that this Faith we call Christian is an altogether suitable traveling companion when we must walk on danger's thin edge.

And, my friend, it seems to me that this is an insight which we who live in our time need more urgently than any generation that has gone before us. It is our lot in our time, to an extraordinary degree, to stand at the edge of the unknown. Of course, the future has always been unknown; but somehow we seem to stand closer to it than our ancestors did. Changes are coming more rapidly now; the pace of everything appears to have accelerated; tomorrow is much less likely to be like today than the tomorrows of our fathers were. Living in this rapidly-changing world, we stand as Joshua stood at the Jordan, and we might well hear, as Joshua's people heard: "Sanctify yourselves . . . for you have not passed this way before."

Thinking with you about a faith for the uncharted way, I have mentioned already the pilgrims and pioneers of early America, the people of the frontier who always stood at the borderline of the unknown. Those were the days of the migrations west, the time of expanding perimeters, the penetration of the wilderness. A while ago I was invited to speak to a meeting of the Daughters of the American Revolution. I began that speech by telling the ladies that I was really ineligible to address them. I said that, in the first place, I was not a daughter of anybody. And I said that, in the second place, when the American Revolutionary War was being fought, my ancestors were already so far into the wilderness that they probably did not know that a war was going on until after it was over.

That early American frontier is memorable in our history: the lone woodsman with his muzzle-loading rifle and powder horn; the scouting party, the covered wagon, the log cabin; Dodge City and Donner Pass; flax fields and spinning wheels; the sound of the woodsman's axe or of *Amazing Grace* sung in common meter beneath the canopy of a brush arbor. That frontier is memorable for the lonely rider and trails blazed from tree to tree, for the hot summers and the cold winters, wild beasts and hostile Indians, "consumption" and typhoid fever and diphtheria — it was not an easy life. It was packed with danger, but with adventure, too. There was a certain romance about it; the fascination of making conquest, of wrestling the wilderness and wresting from it a road by which to go on or a place to call home. That frontier was where a man stood facing the unknown, the comforts of civilization behind him, drawing from it what help he could, but always face to face with what was beyond.

Now all of that is past. And we stand today on a new frontier, at the edge of the new unknown. It isn't geographical; largely, it is ideological. Powerful forces move upon the human mind and spirit. We are engulfed in a cataclysm of change. As Stringfellow Barr has written, "Ours is a world in revolution: if every Communist should commit suicide tomorrow, ours would still be a world in revolution." This is a fact we must accept and face and learn to cope with. New modes and movements sweep the human scene. To many, the old is suspect, and to all, the new is unformed and shapeless. Shrill voices cry, "Down with the establishment," but those voices are not telling us what can be put in the place of it. There is a rising tide of mistrust — mistrust of authority, law, leaders, traditions, and codes of morality. A major motivation is fear, with about half the people afraid things will change and the other half afraid they won't.

But things are going to change; and you can count on that. We have reached the end of the well-trodden trail, the end of the well-marked road, the place where the road abuts the wilderness, and beyond which it does not go on. And this is not a wilderness of trees and mountains and swamps and deserts and animals running wild. This is a wilderness of ideas and attitudes. This is where we are — at the edge of the unknown, on the new frontier; and here we must live, and from here, road or no road, we must go on.

Those other pioneers who wrestled with that other wilderness had a choice: they could move to the frontier, or they could remain in Boston or Philadelphia or New York. The choice was theirs. We have no choice. The frontier on which we live is as wide as the world, as broad as the scope of man's mind, as deep as the human spirit.

Those other pioneers, those of long ago, could retreat; they could go back; they could return to the paved streets and the heated houses and the police protection of the East. But we cannot retreat — not from this frontier. There is nowhere to go; we cannot resign from the human race. We can say, "Stop the world, I want to get off," but the world won't stop. Immediately before World War II a man decided he was fed up with the constant crisis that much of modern living is. So he looked over the map of the world and selected a place to retreat to. That place was an island named Guadalcanal; and if you know the history of World War II, you know what happened there.

That earlier frontier was somewhat local, a place on the map; a person could choose to be there or to be somewhere else. But the frontier on which we live is everywhere, everywhere that man is, and everywhere that mind works — or doesn't work — wherever man thinks or acts, wherever man goes on earth or moon or beyond. In 1885 Horace Greeley looked out from the window of his *New York Tribune* office, saw groups of young fellows loitering on the street, and began to say, "Go west, young man, go west." And the young men did.

And they blew off their pent-up steam coaxing covered wagons across plains and mountains and fixing their dreams on new lands.

But what is the word now? Go west? No; it would be difficult even for Horace Greeley to sell the Los Angeles Freeway as a virgin area offering open arms of opportunity and an invitation to be occupied. Anyone who has driven on that road at rush hour will agree that it's pretty well occupied already! Go where? To restless and adventurous young men — and young women — we can no longer offer the solution of changing geography. The solution must be wrought out in another dimension, a new adventure of mind and spirit. We don't any longer solve anything by just going places, geographically.

That early American frontier disappeared when the Indians were herded like animals onto "reservations," and the forests gave way to the cities, and the buffalo gave their place on the plain to giant combines harvesting grain. This frontier, ours, the one we live on — when will it disappear? Maybe never; because we cannot stand here like planted things at the edge of this unknown; we must move into it; and however far we go, in any moment to which we come, the new frontier will still be standing there before us, a new segment of the seemingly endless jungle forever waiting to be conquered.

May I suggest to you that if we are going to be pioneers and pilgrims on the frontier of our time, we must replace fear with faith. There's no doubt that faith helped the pioneers on that other frontier; but on this frontier, where battles are fought out in the mind and spirit of man, faith is essential. Those earlier pioneers did a pretty good job against the wilderness with axe and rifle and plow. I'm not sure we are doing as well. Perhaps our struggle is not as simple as theirs. We need help; and with all my heart I say this sincerely, although I know some will say it is a cliche and is trite: God is expert in giving help in the very areas we now need it most. *Our*

God is the God of the adventurer, the God of the pilgrim, the God of the pioneer.

The very first call of Christ is "Come, come unto me." Get up and move. Come. And when we arise and respond to that call, we can never know ahead of time all that it may mean. The next call of Christ is "Follow, follow me." Stand up and get going. Through what valleys or rough places or mountain steeps will such following take us before it finally takes us home? We don't know. If the first invitation of Christ is "Come" and if the second one is "Follow," then the very first command which Christ gives to his follower is "Go, go into all the world." Yes, our Lord is the Lord of the pilgrim, and I think he knows how to see us through.

In Hebrews 11:8-10 (R.S.V) we read of God's call to Abraham and of Abraham's response to that call. "By faith Abraham obeyed when he was called to go out to a place which he was to receive as an inheritance; and he went out, now knowing where he was to go. By faith he sojourned in the land of promise, as in a foreign land . . . For he looked forward to the city which has foundations, whose builder and maker is God." Notice the key words here: "When he was called to *go* . . . he *went* . . . not knowing *where*." It was by faith that Abraham obeyed the call and got up and went; and, frankly, it's by faith that anybody gets up and goes anywhere that's worth going.

Pilgrims and pioneers do not move on feet of mistrust and fear. And not only do we need to have faith in the pilgrim's God, but we also need to have some faith in our fellow-pilgrims on the journey. Too much, I believe, we are victims of our own mistrust and suspicion. By these we fence ourselves in. Sometimes younger people say, "Never trust anybody over thirty." Sometimes older people say, "The younger generation is no good." Sometimes we hear, "Never trust a white man." Other times, "Never trust a black man." And some people even say, "Never trust anybody."

Thus we build our high walls and retreat behind them and glare at one another from the ramparts of our fear. You can't be a pilgrim and be like that. You can't be in retreat and be a pioneer at the same time. Understand this: It wasn't fear and mistrust that helped the early American pioneers face the frontier; it was faith and trust and confidence and the kind of courage which is always born of these. And neither will it be fear and mistrust which will make pioneers and pilgrims out of us.

More than three hundred fears, or phobias, are listed in medical dictionaries. There is the fear of darkness and the fear of light. There is the fear of high places and low places. The fear of closed places we call claustrophobia. Some people suffer from pyrophobia, which is the fear of fire, and some from neophobia, which is the fear of what is new. Toxicophobia is the fear of being poisoned, and gamaphobia is the fear of marriage. Pantophobia is the fear of everything; and the person who is not afraid of anything may be suffering from phobophobia, which is the fear of being afraid!

But one of the most devastating of the fears is futurphobia, the fear of the future. It is difficult to go anywhere if you are afraid to take the next step. But if you are walking in faith, trusting your Lord, you don't have to be afraid. He says, "Go . . . and I am with you." Here is one of our Lord's wonderful promises. It is important that we read it correctly. He doesn't say, "Go . . . and I will *go* with you." Rather, he says, "Go . . . and *I am* with you." He is not just a tag-along; he is already out there ahead of us in the very next step we are going to take; and he is there no matter how dark it is.

Near Christmas a few years ago, the Sunday morning bulletin of our church displayed the brightly colored picture of a candle burning among holly leaves, and there was this printed message: "In the darkness shines the everlasting light." When I saw that, I thought of what it means to contemplate a light that is everlasting. The candle will not last forever; in a few hours it will burn away, and its flame will flicker and perish. The kerosene lamps with which I grew up in the Appalachian hills would burn for only a few hours, and then we had to blow out the flame, unscrew the burner, pour in more oil, trim the wick and relight it, and start the whole process over again. Wonderful as electric light bulbs are, one will last only a limited period of time, and then it burns out. And scientists say that the burning sun, the mighty source of light for this whole solar system of ours, is gradually burning itself out, and that at some time in the far-distant future, all its power will be used up and all its light will be gone.

But, isn't it thrilling to know: The Everlasting Light has shined into our darkness, and no matter how long your road may be, or through what it may lead, you can be sure of the Light. That baby born yonder at Bethlehem — a beautiful baby? Yes, I would guess he was. But you may be certain that when he was born he was red and wrinkled as other babies are, and when they held him up by the heels and spanked him, he cried as other babies cry; and you may be certain, too, that, years later, it actually hurt when they drove those large anvil-hammered nails through his hands and feet, and that those were real tears he shed that day when he looked down from the Mount of Olives and beheld the city of Jerusalem and wept over it, and that it was real sweat which fell from his brow that night in the Garden of Gethsemane.

Always remember this: When you go forth on your journey, and he says, "I am with you," you may be certain he has already traveled every road of pain long before your feet ever touch it, and he understands every heartache and every need and is able to turn every shadowed thing into a brightness — and one day he will.

The Jewish people were captives in Babylon, their beloved homeland overthrown, their temple destroyed, the walls of their city thrown to the ground. As we are told in Psalms 137, there by the rivers of Babylon, remembering their homeland, they sat down and wept. They hung their harps on the willows, and their songs of praise were dead in their throats. But there were those among them who dreamed that one day these Babylonian captives would return to the mountains of Judea, that one day they would arise and go home, that they would make the perilous and difficult journey from slavery into freedom again.

One of their prophets told them it would be so. Eloquently he told them that their God was anticipating their journey; God was already in the wilderness preparing the way. Often at Christmas time we read and sing the prophet's inspiring words: "Every valley shall be exalted, and every mountain and hill shall be made low, and the uneven ground shall become smooth, and the rough places plain." (See Isaiah 40:4) Well, as you know, those people, at length, with God's help, did make the journey to Jerusalem.

But they were not the last people to undertake to go somewhere. Others, too, have tried to make the journey from some Babylon to some Jerusalem, out of some servitude into a freedom. And others, too, have learned about the exalting of the valley. Others, too, have discovered, as they have dared to get up and try to go somewhere, that God is out there lifting up the valleys, and leveling down the mountains, and making the rough places plain. No, he doesn't always make the journey easy; but we can be sure of this: as we dare to get up and go, he does always make the journey possible.

But we must venture to move. Those doors designed to open at the command of an electronic eye remain closed unless we walk up to them. If we approach them as though they will open, they do. If we hesitate and hang back as though they won't, they don't. It is an act of faith which opens the door. It is the forward step taken in trust which opens the way to the room which lies beyond.

Do you remember how it was the Israelites, having escaped from Egypt, finally entered into the Promised Land? Having viewed the land from afar, somewhere on the summit of Mount Nebo, Moses had died, and there his body had been buried. The mantle of leadership fell upon Joshua, whose name means "Savior." The Promised Land lay west of the Jordan, and Joshua and his people were east of it, and the Jordan waters were running at flood level. But Joshua lined his people up on the eastward slopes facing west. At the forefront of the assembled column stood the priests of Israel bearing on their shoulders the Ark of the Covenant. Joshua gave the command, "March," and the priest-led column began to move down the hillside to where the swollen waters ran. And strange is the story of what happened then; for it is written that as the feet of the foremost priests touched the water, it rolled back and gave the advancing column a clear passage to the other side (Joshua 3:14-17).

I cannot explain what happened here. But, then, I didn't write the story, and I don't have to explain it. But I know this much about it: it speaks to us the language of a marching and conquering faith. It says to us that we can step with confidence into whatever swollen Jordan may lie before us, and that we can cross with assurance into whatever Promised Land may lie beyond. Here is the faith for the uncharted way, the faith of pilgrims and pioneers.

To Bethlehem and Beyond

Luke 2:1-20
"Let us go . . . and see . . ."

The Christian gospel began at Bethlehem one
star-kissed night when a baby was born, and angels sang,
and shepherds came — when the heavenly Father was so
loving the world that he was giving his Son. To most of
us the outward signals of the Bethlehem Event are
rather well known. We know how shepherds received
from heavenly messengers the announcement of the
birth of Jesus, and how they said, "Let us go to
Bethlehem and see this thing that has happened." We
know how, having made their journey there, those
shepherds "returned, glorifying and praising God for all
that they had seen and heard." It is around these two
actions of the shepherds that I would build the message I
share with you now — their going and their returning.

It is written that these men made known widely the
information they had concerning the newborn Child.
Across the centuries the story of his birth has probably
been more often told than has the story of any other
event in human history. In the course of time there has
grown up around this Event in the Western World a
rather spectacular social phenomenon we call Christmas.
Presumably, Christmas is our way of observing the
Festival of the Birth of Christ. Surrounding this
Bethlehem Event with the Christmas phenomenon as
we have, it sometimes appears that the phenomenon has
engulfed and swallowed up the Event, that the meaning
of the Bethlehem Happening is quite generally obscured
by the tinsels and lights, the scenes and sounds of
Christmas.

It's appropriate to ask this question, I think: How far
are we from Bethlehem? Here, geographically, we may
be some five thousand miles away from that town. Here

at this point in chronological time, we may be nineteen hundred and eighty years away. This may be how far we are away in space and time. But I'm thinking of distance in another dimension. Not in space and time, but in mood and spirit, how far from Bethlehem are we? As God lights the Bethlehem skies with his star, how far are we away from understanding what he wants us to understand? knowing what he wants us to know? feeling what he wants us to feel?

A few Christmases ago, in a somewhat typical American home, the family moved through the chaos of the hurried and harried days of pre-Christmas activity. There was the usual round of parties, shopping, cooking, and getting ready. One member of that family was a little four-year-old girl who was often yelled at, whose playthings, it seemed to her, were always where they shouldn't be, and whose every act, no matter what it was, seemed always to be wrong. Finally, the day before Christmas, when the little one asked some question, her mother's answered was, "Shut up and get out of my way." That night the child knelt at her bedside to offer up The Lord's Prayer. When she reached the place where it says, "Forgive us our trespasses as we forgive those who trespass against us," instead of saying that, she wearily said, "Forgive us our Christmases as we forgive those who Christmas against us."

The mistake of that child may point to some of ours, indicating, it would seem, that we may be a long, long way from the spirit of Bethlehem. In a large department store, crowded with Christmas shoppers, a young husband was overheard impatiently saying to his wife, "What do you want me to do, stand on my head?" A few years ago *The Saturday Review of Literature* published a modern parable, written as though it were a story from a local newpaper: "Last night John Elzy, watchman at the Grand Eagle Department Store, while making his rounds of the bargain basement, found the body of a man lying under a counter. He was thin to the point of emaciation, apparently in his middle thirties, and was shabbily dressed. His pockets were empty and there were no marks of identification upon his person. Store officials believe that he was trampled in the Christmas rush and crawled under the counter for shelter. But they are unable to account for what appear to be nail wounds in his hands." Christ trampled in the Christmas rush! It's a terribly disturbing picture. But I'm afraid there are elements of truth in it.

In *The Genius and the Goddess* by Aldous Huxley, the narrator sees his guest to the door as he is leaving on Christmas Eve, and his parting words are: "Drive carefully; this is a Christian country, and this is the Savior's birthday; practically everybody you meet will be drunk." It is, of course, a matter of record that in our country, in the three weeks around Christmas, more liquor is drunk and more people are killed than at any other time in the entire year. Somehow it seems incongruous and inappropriate, doesn't it?

There are many in our society who have no idea what Christmas is really supposed to mean. Historically ignorant and spiritually insensitive, having clothed themselves in the mantle of secularism, they apparently are unable to see anything beyond it. A well-dressed modern young couple, apparently of some refinement and culture, stood at the window of a large big-city department store. Displayed in the window was a replica of the Bethlehem stable scene, with shepherds, wise men, Joseph, Mary, and the Child in the manger. The young woman was heard saying, "Why did they put that baby in that window, and why did they put it in a thing like that?"

Just before Christmas the carolers had set up their street altar and were singing there. One man, walking by, said to the man walking with him, "Look there, would you; now these Christians are even trying to take over Christmas." The poor fellow exposed his abysmal ignorance in putting the historical cart in front of the historical horse. Christmas? The Christians had it first. We were singing, "Joy to the world; the Lord is come; let earth receive her King," long before anybody ever sang "Frosty the Snow Man" or "Rudolph, the Red-nosed Reindeer." The carolers singing on the street weren't trying to take over Christmas from anybody; they were simply laying claim to what was already rightfully and properly theirs.

How far are we from Bethlehem? I have the uneasy feeling that many of us have a long way to go. Peace and good will among men? On the human scene there's a tragic lot of glaring at one another, and screaming, and the unintelligible sounds of blind conflict. Well, the shepherds said, "Let us go now to Bethlehem and see this thing that has happened there." This Christmas, let's try to join them; let's go. It will be a journey made in mind and spirit, a pilgrimage of heart and soul and mood, a journey we make in the world within.

Let us arise and go — out of our blase and well-practiced atheism, out of our blatant commercialism, our selfish egotism, our enslaving preoccupation with lesser things. It will be a long journey, for the world it may require a long time; but it is a journey an individual person can make in five minutes.

If we, now, are to go and see, as shepherds, then, went and saw, it will not be a baby in a manger that we shall find. We will have to look beyond the infant and the virgin mother. We'll have to go farther, and see. We'll have to see his virgin life, hear his vital word, behold his vicarious death, and understand his victorious resurrection. For we can know the meaning of what happens at Bethlehem only if we can see it in the light of what happens later — at places like Gethsemane and Calvary and the Easter Garden — and out in the world where Christ has touched our human life here and there, now and again, for almost two thousand years.

Places where great persons were born are sometimes marked with monuments; those monuments are never erected on the day of the birth, but later in the light of passing time. I have stood, as you probably have, at Hodgenville, Kentucky, before the beautiful memorial which marks the birthplace of Abraham Lincoln. That monument was not erected on February 12, 1809, but after Springfield, and Cooper Union, and Gettysburg, and the Emancipation Proclamation, and Ford's Theater — after time had put Lincoln to the test which it alone can administer.

Imagine this scene, if you will. On February 22, 1732, a planter from down the Potomac returns from an up-river errand, and says to his wife, "This has been a great day in American history, for today little George Washington was born." Well, that's a scene you must imagine, because it didn't happen, and it never could. For the world never knew of Washington's greatness until it was seen exemplified in the years of his life, the function of his mind, and the deeds of his hand. I'm saying, my friend, that if you want to go to Bethlehem, in mind and spirit, to inbreathe the meaning of what happens there, you musn't end your journey at that mangerside; you must go on and see the Child in the full light and power of all he was. He was not just another baby.

Here we are today almost two thousand years this side of the Bethlehem Event, standing in the full light of all that has come between then and now. Most of us think we are fairly secure; we are reasonably comfortable; and we are likely to say, "Well, it's Christmas again, period." But that's not quite enough. We need to remember that Magi *arose* and followed a star, that shepherds *arose* and went when angels sang. So let us *arise* — out of our indifference and insensitivity, our preoccupation with trinkets and trifles. Let us go — beyond the boundaries of narrow horizons, go to where we've never been before. Let us see — more deeply and more completely than we've ever seen.

It's a journey we need to make, a pilgrimage of spirit our hearts desperately need to undertake. Our altar fires burn low, and we need a place of rekindling, of warming again, and this journey's destination is that place. Our souls are depleted with trials and struggles, and we need a place of refilling, and this is that place. Our spirits sag and droop with disappointments, and we need the reawakening of dream, a revival and renewal, and Bethlehem appears before us like a green oasis before the desert traveler after the long, long march. Phillips Brooks was right: "The world has grown old under its burden of care, but at Christmas it is always young." At least it ought to be.

We live in a world of dangerous complexities. Near Baltimore, Maryland, a few years ago, one of our fast military planes fired its guns at a make-believe target straight ahead, overtook its own bullets in flight, and shot itself down. Often we are laden with burdens that wear our lives away. During a lull in a World War II battle, a thirty-five year old American soldier wearily said to his buddy, "This is a young man's war." His nineteen year old buddy sighed and said, "Yes, I suppose it is; but as soon as you're in it, you aren't young any more." There is a lot of darkness around us; and often many of us have felt like the small boy at bedtime who said, as the babysitter turned out the light, "There's too much darkness in this room."

Let me say it again: We need, so urgently need, to make pilgrimage to Bethlehem, where heaven bends down to touch the hurt of earth, and where God lays six or eight pounds of infant Child amid the darkness, and a halo of light is formed, and grows, and grows, and grows until *he* says, "I am the light of the world." A small boy's father died, and the little fellow was lonely for his dad. For long hours at a time, he would sit on the living room floor before his father's picture which hung above the fireplace mantel. One day, sitting there, hungrily looking up, he said to his mother, "Mommy, I wish daddy could step down out of the picture."

Our heavenly Father has; he has stepped down out of the picture. Jehovah has become Immanuel; God is with us. He has stepped into our darkness and loneliness. He has come all the say. He didn't stop at Bethlehem where he was born, or at Gethsemane where he suffered, or at Calvary where he died, or even at the opened tomb from which he came forth alive. He said, "My Father has sent me," and he didn't stop until he had gotten himself all the way to us, and can say, "Behold, I stand at the door and knock."

Imagine this drama, if you will. The scene is your home; the time is just before Christmas. There is a gay tree, a jolly Santa, and holly and pine and mistletoe and light. The days pass, and then it's Christmas Day. The children are out of their beds early; there are toys and goodies and new things. Then everybody comes — grandpa and grandma, uncles and aunts, and cousins from all around. The house is filled with the fragrance of good cooking, and with laughter and excitement. Then all sit at the great table, filled with all good things; and just at that moment *the doorbell rings.*

"Now who can that be?" someone says, "Who would be out on Christmas Day?" Someone goes and opens the door — and there stands a Man — a strange Man — a quietly strange Man. All turn and look at him, and suddenly every voice is still. Every eye is on him, and all are transfixed by what they see.

This Man at the door — who is he? He wears the garments of an ancient Palestinian shepherd, but his shoes are the wooden shoes of the Netherland Lowlands; he is stooped as a laborer in the cottonfields of the American South, but his skin is bronzed and dark as one who has braved the icy blasts of the Northland; his hands, although scarred, are the sensitive and delicate hands of an artist or a surgeon; his eyes are slanted slightly as a man from the distant East, but his voice is heavy with the accent of central Europe, yet somehow light with the music of the Pacific Islands.

All eyes are upon him – and instantly every person *knows exactly who he is.* He belongs to the world, this Christ. He has come to us — all the way. But if the meaning of this is to come alive in us, we must go, we must arise and go; like shepherds of old, we must go and see; we must "see this which is come to pass, which the Lord has made known unto us." (Luke 2:15). But the point I would make is this; we don't have to travel one thousand nine hundred and eighty years through time; he is with us *now.* We don't have to travel five thousand miles through space; he is with us *here.* And the journey to which I summon you is a journey of mind and spirit, a journey you make deep within yourself, a journey you can better make on your knees than on your feet.

But we cannot camp forever at Bethlehem; we must go on from there. He did; and if we are to follow him, we must. Bethlehem is merely the first stop on a longer journey. Here at the Bethlehem station we pause to equip our spirits with reverence, sharpen our sense of wonder, get new wings for our faltering hopes, and lift up our eyes for going on. As from Bethlehem Jesus went on to his life, so from Bethlehem we must go on to ours.

The shepherds went away from Bethlehem glorifying and praising God and telling what they had seen and heard. Surely they took away with them something they hadn't brought. A new dimension of experience had been added. As their Bethlehem pilgrimage made a difference to them, ours should make a difference to us. We are told that the Magi, having been to Bethlehem, "returned to their own country another way" (Matthew 2:12). I doubt if shepherds or Magi were ever quite the same again. And if you and I, in the venture of living, can make it as far as Bethlehem, I am sure it will make a difference in all the rest of the journey we make.

You see, here at Bethlehem God is saying something to us. At this juncture on the journey, he is giving us a signal for going on. Here he speaks in a language which is uniquely his own, a language in which he had never spoken before and in which he has not spoken since. Across the centuries the message has produced its reverberations and its echoes, but in the language with which God spoke here he has spoken only once. Half a century or so after the Bethlehem Event, one of the New Testament writers put it this way: "God, who at various times, and in many ways, spoke in time past unto our fathers by the prophets, has in these last days spoken unto us by his Son" (Hebrews 1:1-2).

This, in my opinion, is one of the most dynamic declarations to be found anywhere in our Christian Scriptures. It is saying that the God who has spoken many times has now spoken again. It is saying that the God who has spoken to others has now spoken to us. And it is saying that the God who has spoken in many ways has now spoken in the living language of "word made flesh" to "dwell among us" (John 1:14).

Indeed it had been in widely varied ways that God had spoken in the times that had gone by. He had thundered forth his law until the rocks shook and the mountain smoked at Sinai, and thus he had spoken to Moses. But he had spoken differently to Elijah at Mount Horeb; there his word was not in the earthquake, nor in the wind that rent the mountains, nor in the fire that seared the land, but in "the still small voice" that came after the earthquake and the wind and the fire had passed. His voice had been heard by Jacob in a dream, by Job from a whirlwind, and by Isaiah from the temple altar.

And, of course, after the Bethlehem Event the voice of God has been heard by others as he has spoken in other varied ways from places with names such as Jerusalem and Galilee, and Gethsemane and Calvary. But only once has he ever spoken as he spoke that star-lit night at Bethlehem. Here he uttered himself as at no other time; here he expressed himself as at no other place. Here his word assumed a form it has taken only once. He wrapped up all there was of love and goodness and grace and life-lifting power in the person of an infant man-child, and laid him in a manger.

Here he gave his only Son (John 3:16). He never gave another. Here he spoke in terms of a living person. Here his language was uniquely his own. And, my dear friend, if you and I are to receive the message of Bethlehem, we are going to have to learn the language of God. Until we learn it, the signals that come from Bethlehem fall upon our ears as the strange sounds of a foreign tongue. If we are going to learn the language in which God speaks at Bethlehem, we must first of all clearly understand that it is intensely and ultimately personal. God is saying what he is saying not in the abstract terms of philosophy, or in the concrete terms of science, but in the personal terms of life, and of love, and relationship.

I think we should look a little at this. Usually we don't protest greatly when fellowship is communicated in personal ways. Normally, a fellow who thinks a lot of his girl friend would rather go to see her than to call her up on the telephone. "I love you" said in person on a moonlit night is generally more desirable than the same three words typed in a letter and sent from a thousand miles away. I know of no philosophy that can substitute for a handclasp, and certainly no science. If you have ever walked through some shadowed valley of sorrow, you know that it means much more for someone to draw near and walk with you, than for a whole multitude to stand aloof and give lectures on how to do it.

Goethe gives us a priceless insight when he writes: "To know how cherries and strawberries taste, you must ask the children and the birds." French essayist Montaigne once wrote: "If anyone should ask me to give a reason why I loved my friend, there could be only one answer: Because he was he, and I was I." Yes, we know, don't we, that the personal values are the best ones. And God knows this, too; he knew it long before we did. And when he wished to say his ultimate word, he spoke in the language of a living person, the Living Person of Jesus Christ.

But I must raise this question with you: Have we got the message? When Jesus was born, and angels sang, there must have been thousands of persons within hearing range, but apparently only a few heard. When Jesus was born, and the star shone, there must hve been hundreds of thousands in position to see, but apparently only a few saw. At one point, near the close of his earthly life, while Jesus was talking with his disciples, Philip asked him a question, a question which revealed the questioner was not as well informed concerning the identity of Jesus as a good disciple should have been. Jesus patiently answered: "Have I been with you so long, and yet you do not know me, Philip?" (John 14:9 R.S.V.) Apparently there was much for Philip yet to learn. The message hadn't yet gotten through to him, not really.

Do you recall that episode in the banquet hall of Belshazzar, King of Babylon? It was during the captivity of the Jewish people there, and the king was having a gigantic party, a mammoth banquet for the more important lords of the realm. During the festivities, they drank wine from the sacred vessels they had taken from the temple in Jerusalem when they had overthrown the city. It must have been quite a wingding; but in the midst of it, so the story goes, there came forth the finger of a man's hand, and wrote upon the wall: "Mene, Mene, Tekel Upharsin." The message really was this: "God has numbered your kingdom and finished it; you are weighed in the balances and found wanting; the kingdom is divided and given to the Medes and Persians." But the proud king was unable to read a word that was written; he just didn't know the language. He had to call the Jewish prophet Daniel to tell him what it meant (Daniel 5:1-28). Many times God is saying something and the addressee just doesn't get the message. Many times we just don't know the language in which he speaks.

Do you recall that episode on the Mesopotamian plain when a group of ancient people undertook to build a tower that would reach all the way up to heaven? It was called the tower of Babel. God tried to tell those people how stupid they were; but they didn't hear him. And quite soon they weren't hearing each other either. There was a confusion of tongues. They didn't get the message from God, and they couldn't get messages to one another. Nobody could understand anybody else; they were unable to work together; and the tower they started was never finished.

Once, in the teaching career of Jesus, he had led his disciples into the presence of truth they had never encountered before. He had led them like pilgrims to the pioneer edge of things. There, perplexed and puzzled, half believing and half disbelieving, they looked at one another in awed wonder. And it is written: "They did not understand what he said, and they were afraid to ask him what he meant" (Mark 9:32). At this point I think what I want to say is this: When we learn the language of God, we'd better be prepared for some kind of revelation.

I doubt if God deals in inanities. When he speaks, we should expect something more than small talk. What will the revelation be? It may be, as it was to Belshazzar, that you cannot build a kingdom that will last very long if you build it on slavery, brutality, and other people's blood. It may be as it was to the builders at Babel, that you cannot build a tower that will reach to heaven, or to anywhere else of importance, if you cannot communicate with your fellow-builders and work together in the building. Or the revelation may be, as our Lord would have it be for all humankind, that "God was in Christ, reconciling the world unto himself" (2 Corinthians 5:19). What the message in any circumstance will be, I cannot predict; but I think I'm safe in saying that when we get to the point of understanding the language of God, there'll be a message.

And we need it. With all our follies and frustrations, we certainly need some message of help and guidance.

An interesting little gag type of gadget is being marketed in some parts of our country. It is a pocket-sized case marked on the outside with the words "Mariner's Compass." When opened, all that is seen inside is a small mirror in which the opener sees his own reflection. And printed there is this explanatory sentence: "This won't tell you which way to go, but it will show you who is lost." That doesn't, of course, add immensely to our fund of knowledge; but in a whimsical way it does suggest we need help.

Many of us know what it is like to encounter frustration and meet disappointment around almost every corner. We know what it is like to try and fail, to live with the ghosts of dead dreams and with other dreams which are barely alive and won't quite consent to die. We can understand the feeling expressed by Sam Walter Foss in these lines:

On the thirty-second day of the thirteenth month
Of the eighth day of the week,
On the twenty-fifth hour of the sixty-first minute,
We'll find all the things that we seek.

Someone has said of H. G. Wells that he spent forty years of his life saying with total finality, "I am persuaded that neither life nor death, nor angels, nor principalities, nor powers, nor height nor depth, nor anything else in all creation, shall be able to separate me from the power of *science.*" But the last thing that Wells wrote before his death was a pessimistic, gloomy, and despairing book entitled *Mind at the End of Its Tether.* O how desperately humankind needs to learn the language of God.

We deeply hunger, most of us, for some word from beyond. We can understand the outcry of Zophar the Naamathite when, in conversation with the suffering Job, he exclaimed, "O that God would speak" (Job 11:5). Most of us from time to time have reason to know what Tennyson meant when he wrote:

What am I? An infant crying in the night,
An infant crying for the light,
And with no language but a cry.

There is a precious story of a seven year old boy who stood by the crib of new newborn baby brother, and said, "Tell me quick before you forget: what is God like?" So much do we yearn for some communication from him.

Tennyson was essentially right: we have no language but a cry; but we do have that, and I think God hears it. God, however, does have a language. His language is more than words and requires more than ears to hear. We don't exactly comprehend the language of God in the same way we may overhear a casual remark made in the office elevator. Someone has said that fellowship is more than a coffee break. It is; and communication is more than the production and hearing of sounds.

I heard about a fellow who, on his way home from work one evening, realized that he hadn't for a long time told his wife how he felt about her. He made up his mind that he would do so that very night. So after the dinner dishes were cleared away, and the two of them were seated in their living room, he behind his newspaper and she with her magazine, he lowered his paper a trifle, looked over it in her direc27on and said, "I love you." Without lowering her magazine, she replied somewhat absently, "Yes, I know; and I'm tired of you, too!" There are some kinds of communication for which the stage must be set. I suspect this fellow would have gotten a better response had he set the stage before he spoke.

Well, at Bethlehem God has set the stage, and from that stage he speaks. But if we are to understand what he says, we are under the necessity of tuning out a lot of discordant sounds, and tuning in the voice that speaks the message of forgiving and redeeming love in the personal language of heaven's "unspeakable gift" to us. The language of love is, most deeply, extra-verbal; and it arises from somewhere beyond and below the vocal cords, and it is received somewhere in the heart-regions of life beyond the reach of mind. What God is saying is person-to-person. The communication he initiates is not exactly a long-distance station-to-station call. Communication is always difficult, and sometimes impossible, unless there is a common language. And the message which comes from Bethlehem is spoken in the language of a living and loving Person giving himself. And I think we'll learn this language only as we become living and loving persons giving ourselves.

Not every language is understood equally well in all situations. Did you ever hear the story of the farmer who drove his wagon and mule team to town? He returned home very, very late that night, much later than he normally should have. His wife wanted to know why he was so late, and his explanation was this: "I started at the usual time, but on my way I overtook the preacher. He was walking, so I picked him up and let him ride with me; and from that time on those mules never understood one word I said." Apparently the language he had taught them to understand was not an all-purpose one. When he had to trim from it what he didn't want the preacher to hear, it didn't impress the mules at all.

I have tried to say here that, like the shepherds, we need to arise and go — in mood and spirit — to Bethlehem. I have tried to say that we need to learn the language in which God is speaking there. And why do I say these things? Because there at Bethlehem God has established Contact Point One, and we need to meet him there. Changing the figure from that of the military to that of the ocean voyager, there at Bethlehem God has made his first landfall. In the momentous divine incursion into our world, there at Bethlehem are seen the first signals of what it means.

If you were God, and if you wanted to communicate your love to all of humankind, how would you do it? Would you stand on a cloud and say, "World, I love you?" I doubt it — not unless you want to be invited to join a circus. Would you do a lot of nice things for humanity and list them all in a great big book, and have it notarized, and say, "Look, world, I am hereby proving my love?" I doubt it — not unless you want to create a great mass of lazy dependents who will line up at your door waiting for you to do your next nice thing. Would you always reach out and rescue every wandering human who is just about to fall over a precipice, or stumble into a pit, or fall on his face, or get into trouble, or get his life all loused up? I doubt it — not unless you want all your people to spend their time playing on the brink of some disaster because they know that you won't let them really get hurt.

I repeat: If you were God, and if you wanted to communicate your love to all of humankind, how would you do it? Well, you aren't God, and I'm glad you aren't; God is God, and I'm glad he is. And he has wanted to communicate his love to all of humankind, and he does want to do it. And what he has done and does is the greatest venture in communication this world has ever seen. The only trouble is that much of the world has not really seen it.

In our time we hear a lot about communication, about person getting through to person, about our understanding one another. There's a lot of concern about a true conveyance of thoughts and feelings, about bridging gulfs between persons, about getting past the high walls that so much divide us. We have many kinds of communicaton devices; we don't send messages by tom-tom relay or pony express any more. A word can be sent around the world in a flash. There are more ways than ever before to get a word from person to person or group to group.

Yet, with frightening frequency, one person or group says to another: "You are not hearing me." The implication is that one is listening to words, but not hearing what is meant. I think Jesus encountered the problem of getting through to people with his meanings, and that he knew the problem well. After all, again and again he had occasion to say, "He who has ears to hear, let him hear." Each person to whom Jesus spoke had attached to his head a couple of physical blobs called ears; Jesus wasn't suggesting these were absent from some heads; but he was saying that some people weren't getting the message. How is it, he asks, that "having ears, you do not hear?" Jesus knew the problem long before we did.

The problem is, in part at least, that we are so much preoccupied with what we are already thinking that we cannot accommodate anything new or different. Sometimes we are so sure we know ahead of time what is going to be said that we do not hear it when it is. We are often so tuned in on our pre-selected wavelengths that we cannot adjust to receive anything that comes through on another channel. And, in our time especially, besieged as we are with an electronic bombardment of verbiage, we have so often listened to so many words that meant nothing, that we do not expect the next ones to mean any more.

I'm sure God must run into all these problems in trying to communicate with us. Communication is a hazardous enterprise. No, it's usually not a grave problem to tell someone the time of day; but the communication of *ideas* is another matter. One preacher said that the way to preach is to tell the people you are going to tell them, then tell them, and then tell them you told them! As any preacher knows well, even all of that sometimes isn't enough. One university professor put it this way: "I know what lecture I give, but I am never sure what lecture my students hear." This is the first hazard of trying to communicate: the risk of being misunderstood. And if we sometimes think we have difficulty getting others to understand the relatively simple things we talk about, how very great must be God's problem in getting us to hear the majestic and unprecedented thing that he would say to us. And he is saying it — not so much in the language of words as in the language of a Living Person.

A second hazard of communication is the risk of getting hurt; and when you are trying to communicate love, that risk is enormously large. Loving is the soul's supreme adventure. When you truly love, something of you is going forth, venturing out into the life of another, or into the lives of others, becoming vulnerable. When you love, you turn yourself inside out, and expose your inner heart to the hazards of whatever may happen. Sometimes, concerning helpfulness to others, someone says, "I won't put myself out." But when you love, you do. And at Behtlehem God is loving.

Someone has said, "It's a risk to put your love out to anyone." But God takes that risk. He has put his love out to everyone. Don't overlook the fact that it was "his own *beloved* Son" whom he gave (John 3:16). And he got hurt. It may seem somehow improper to say this; but we'll never understand the meaning of his loving act until we understand that in his putting himself out for us, God got hurt. There was a crown of thorns, and a cross, and the pain of nails in hands and feet — and the deeper pain of being rejected by those whom he loved.

But, if we can accept it, it is through his pain that we have our peace, it is "by his stripes that we are healed" (Isaiah 53:5). Because he gave, we may receive. Out of his sorrow comes our joy — and also his. For he is "the pioneer and perfecter of our faith, who for the joy that was set before him, endured the cross" (Hebrews 12:2). His joy is to be our Savior; and if there is pain in the process of getting through to us, there is joy when he does.

What was the message heard by shepherds that night in the fields of Bethlehem? "Unto you is born this day in the city of David a Savior who is Christ the Lord" (Luke 2:11). It was the simple announcement of the coming and presence of a living Person. May we make pilgrimage of mind and spirit until we are within hearing range of this declaration — and may we know who he is.

A number of years ago a group of British noblemen

were gathered in London when the king of Great Britain entered the room. All of them knew him personally as a man; yet all honored him as their king. When he entered, they all solemnly stood to their feet. "Take your seats, gentlemen," said the king, "I count you as personal friends." Then, somewhat jokingly, he added, "I am not the Lord, you know." Whereupon, one of the men, a true Christian at heart, said to the king, "No, sir, you aren't; and if you were our Lord, we would not stand on our feet; we would fall on our knees."

The Light that Shines Within

John 1:1-18
"The light shines in the darkness . . ."

The story of the birth of Jesus has been variously told. Luke has told it in relation to the appearance of angels and the visit of shepherds. Matthew has told it in the context of a brightly shining star and the coming of wise men from the East. Others may very well have associated the story with other signal happenings mentioned by neither of these; for any event of importance is attended by a variety of incidental circumstances, and in telling of it, one witness will choose to relate one of the incidentals and another will relate a different one. The whole story is learned as everyone is heard.

In the New Testament it is John more than any other who undertakes to tell us what really happened at Bethlehem. He is saying that God was so loving the world that he was giving his own Son (John 3:16). And here in the prologue to the Gospel which bears John's name we have a supreme philosophical setting-forth of that incomparable Event. The Word was becoming flesh (1:14). The light was shining into the darkness (1:5). The true light that enlightens every man was coming into the world (1:9). John does not deal at all with outward circumstance. He paints no word pictures portraying sight or sound. He writes of the inward realities of which the sights and sounds were the outward signs.

But there is no way to speak of spiritual and metaphysical reality without some use of physical image. To convey a metaphysical truth, we must choose a word picture which represents it, then paint that picture with the brushstrokes of language, and hope our listeners will be able to translate it into the meaning which we intended. And this, in a most masterful manner, John does in the prologue to this Gospel. "The light shines into the darkness!" This is the figure of speech by which John would convey to us the profound truth of what was actually happening that night at Bethlehem.

Now let's look at what it means. "The light" — certainly this encompasses all of God's care and good intention and love for us. The light "shines" — it is emitted, it comes forth. "Into the darkness." now what's that? Too often we have some vague notion about some nebulous kind of darkness — out yonder somewhere — which is penetrated by a light. Not so. The darkness is within us; it is an aspect of our personhood. It is into this darkness the light comes, into this moral and spiritual shadow-land of our own minds and souls. The "light" is the very personal forthcoming of him in whom "the whole fullness of the deity dwells." (Colossians 2:9). The "darkness" is the very personal inner space of our own very human lives. It is into this darkness the light is come.

I think we are made for the light, meant for it, and it for us. It is of much interest to me to read the Old Testament book of Genesis and realize that before God said, "Let us make man," he said, "Let there be light." The indication is that he put his man into a lighted world. But somehow we got all mixed up with darkness, and our inner selves were infiltrated and flooded by it.

But let's be careful now that we do not sell ourselves short. Much darkness as there is within us, don't you think God saw something in us that was worth coming for? reaching for? The darkness within us conceals much that is beautiful and of precious worth. God knows the beauty and the value are there; he can see them through the shadows. And so, comes the light, that the darkness may be driven away and the beauty shine forth. So, to start with now, let's think together about you and me, the wonderful world within us, the inner world of what we are.

We live in a wonderful world. We may look to the east and see the sunrise, to the west and see the sunset;

we may listen to the song of birds and the whisper of wind. We may go out in the springtime into the orchard or the flower garden and experience life; we may smell the fragrance of lilac or the aroma of moss on a mountain rock. We may observe the seasons as they change, feel the changing moods of day and night, know the melancholy of rain, the peace of a twilight, or the expectant hush of the dawn. We may lift our eyes and look upon the stars, the vast galaxies and the deep of space. We may behold the mystery and wonder of light. We may travel to distant places and view the mighty mountains, the wide seas, the deep jungles and fertile plains and fields of growing grain. We may let our gaze sweep the earth and behold the marvels of man's creative genius, the great structures and machines, the ships that sail the sea and air and go even where the air is not.

Yes, it's out there — the wonderful world we live *in*. We may travel to see it, reach to touch it. But there is another world, the world within, the world of what we are, the world of the inner heart. It is the world of deepest hunger and longing, of highest aspiration and dream, the world of struggle and quest, the world of feelings too deep for words. It is the world where everything that has meaning must at least give account of itself.

The human body is wonderful — with its systems, checks and balances, thermostats and controls and communicaton devices. But it is not these of which I would speak. I speak of the world you *are*, not of the body you have, nor of the world *in* which you live, but of the world of what you are — a world of joy and sorrow, pleasure and pain, the inner world where great emotions surge and ebb like ocean tides, a world of deep awarenesses where profound sensibilities are. The Old Testament psalmist declared, "I am fearfully and wonderfully made" (139:14). He was. And so are you.

When the psalmist said that, he wasn't thinking of body parts, of stomach and lungs and pituitary glands, wonderful as all these are. He was thinking, I believe, of all that happens in the inner world in a lifetime of years. There is the rosy glow of childhood, with fancies and fairies, and the slow dawning of insight, and growing pains. There is the romance of early adulthood, reachings and yearnings, the search for identity, the realization of love and struggle. There is the adventure of the creative years; then the nostalgia of advancing age. And through it all there is laughter and there are tears and the intricate criss-cross of lights and shadows that form their ever-changing patterns over the landscape of the swiftly passing years.

Yes, it's a wonderful world, this world within. Feeling its wonder, the psalmist in great excitement spoke to his own soul: "Bless the Lord, O my soul; and all that is within me, bless his holy name!" (103:1) *All that is within me!* How much is that? We get a little glimpse here and there, a little bit of suggestion now and then. Who knows, really? Who can imagine? Remember that boy baby who was born at Hodgenville, Kentucky, on February 12, 1809? He was born in poverty, without privilege as the world measures privilege, in circumstances we tend to look on in our day as wholly dependent upon society and without productive quality.

But what was in him — that Lincoln lad? Young Abe reading borrowed books by firelight, what was in him? I doubt if any neighbor suspected or imagined. Edwin Markham wrote: "The color of the ground was in him, the smack and tang of elemental things." But there was more. I suppose no one would ever have known it was there had it not come out; but it did. Sometimes it comes out, and sometimes it doesn't; but it's in there — this wonderful world of the inner heart.

It's wonderful in its capacity. There is the ability to love. All the human love that is anywhere is in there, not out there in the world of things. It's wonderful also in its potential to be bright and beautiful or dark and dismal. And there's nothing out there that has meaning until it means something in here. Here is the ultimate proving ground of all values. Things are of no worth in themselves. They are worthless unless they add to the world within, unless they can become instruments to add content, quality, enrichment, resources of power, and wellsprings of peace.

Thomas Gray wrote: "Many a rose blooms to blush unseen and waste its fragrance on the desert air." I believe God enjoys a rose, and every blooming rose is therefore a thing of value. But so far as we human creatures are concerned, the rose is a thing without worth unless a human spirit is able to receive and be enriched and inspired by its beauty. A treasure of sunsets, a fortune in starlight — these but pass away in waste if there is no human spirit in which they can invest themselves, and be translated into spiritual quality, and so achieve a kind of immortality. And, as everyone knows, a fortune in stocks and bonds can be a misfortune unless it can add quality and content to the inner spirit of him who has it in possession and to the inner spirits of those around him. Someone says: "We live in deeds, not years; in thoughts, not breaths; in feelings, not in figures on a dial; and we should count time by heartthrobs."

I have been trying to illustrate for you the immense dimension and importance of the wonderful world of inner spirit. Now let me say: it is into this world that the light shines. God knows where his light is needed most — and where it will do the most good, where it will make the most difference. So he beams his light into our darkness, revealing the beauty that is there.

I wish to say two or three things about the coming and presence of the light. And the first one is: *It is in this light that we should see our own life.* I strongly feel that one reason that light is come is to illuminate our own view of what we are. Many times it makes an important difference in what light we see things. Physically, we can illustrate this in a wide variety of ways.

My wife and I visited one of the famous caverns of America. There, deep beneath the earth's surface, time and nature had carved spectacular formations of artistic design and beauty. As we stood watching these, the light upon them changed, moving through a series of colors and combinations. As the light changed, the formations appeared to change also. In one light they were witches' castles, eerie and shadowed; but in another light they were like great temples gleaming in the sun. Perhaps you have seen cave illumination of this kind, and perhaps, too, you have seen a delicately beautiful show called Dancing Waters. The performers are simply streams and sprays of water jettisoned upward and outward from a series of nozzles. An enchanting effect is produced by the varied coloring and slanting of the lights that play upon them.

A few years ago, while on a church mission in southern California, I was driven by a friend after dark to the home of some fine folks who were to be my host and hostess for a few days. In the darkness I knew the road we traveled had climbed somewhat; but it was not until the morning sun drove away the darkness that I could see where I was — on an inspiring hilltop, with an orange grove for a front yard, overlooking the city of Camarillo and a wide expanse of the Pacific ocean. Yes, light makes a fantastic different.

In what light do you see your life, yourself? Your doorbell rings; you open the door; and before you stands a man of disheveled appearance who is asking you for a "buck" so, as he says, he can buy a sandwich. His whole life perspective is limited to one immediate problem: Where is his next meal coming from? He is not interested in the sunset which gleams golden in the west behind him. He is unaware of the tulips that bloom there by his feet. He is not at all impressed with the heights and ranges and reaches of mind and spirit. He sees all there is of his life in the light of the hunger pain he feels in his stomach. I well remember the time such a man approached me on a Cincinnati street and said the usual thing: "Mister, can you spare a dime?" That was before inflation and certain other changes after which such people usually ask for dollars rather than dimes. My response to this man was: "My friend, is it a dime you really need?" In my heart I was saying to him: Is it a dime you deeply want? Will a dime solve your problem? Will it fulfill your life? It is enough? And then I said to him, "Why don't you ask for a million dollars?" Of course, that wouldn't have solved his problem either; I knew that, and so did he — I think. Life is sometimes seen in a tiny pinpoint of light, and that very dim.

A woman in a hospital with a pain in her side is facing surgery tomorrow. She is prone to see all of life in the light of that immediate circumstance. She is likely to forget the immeasurable value of the love with which she is surrounded. She may not be aware of all the good things life has brough to her up to this time; it may seem to her now that never in her life has she ever seen a golden sunrise. And the little pinpoint of light in which she sees things is just not big enough or bright enough. I observe a man's picture in the newspaper. He is a billionaire. His face is a mask, the unreadable face of the proverbial poker player. The word is that he has this week swallowed up another giant corporation. I look at his picture with a mixture of anxiety and pity. He may be a broad and deep and balanced man; but I somehow doubt if he is. He is very likely to see his life only in the light of an impassioned craving for more, to see himself only as a juggler of dollar signs and a manipulator of people.

The wife and small son of a certain storekeeper sat by a window one evening looking at the stars and talking about heaven. The little fellow asked his mother, "Will I go to heaven?" She said, "Yes." And the boy said, "Will you?" and she replied that she would, too. There was a long silence; and then the child said, "But Daddy won't, will he?" "Why?" his mother replied, "Why do you say that?" And the little one sadly answered, "Because Daddy won't be able to get away from the store." O yes he will — he'll get away from the store all right. The time will come; he'll get away, there's no question about that. But even the child knew something about his dad: that he was living in a narrowly limited portion of himself. The man was seeing his life in a pathetic little pinpoint of light, and he wasn't seeing all of it.

Well, of course we all see our life in the light of something. And often that light is not big enough, bright enough, good enough, or total enough. Many dim views of life are going around; for many are the people who do not see life in a light that is at all clear. To some, life is simply biological; man is just an animal, a beast — resourceful and imaginative, but a beast nonetheless. To some, life is futile, without point, purpose, or goal. To some, life is a pre-determined product of circumstance and nothing more. But Jesus said, "Your life is more than" you thought it was. And, my friend, usually it is. So, in the coming of the light, God is doing something about this: He is trying to help us see.

Now listen to one of the great passages of Holy Scripture; listen to what God has done, and what God intends. These words are from Paul's second letter to Timothy, chapter one: "Never be ashamed of your testimony to our Lord ... It is he who brought us salvation, and called us to a dedicated life, not for any merit of ours, but of his own purpose and grace, which was granted us in Christ Jesus from all eternity, but has *now at length* been brought *fully into view* by the *appearance on earth* of our Savior Jesus Christ. For he *has broken the power of death* and *brought life and immortality to light through the Gospel*" (2 Timothy 1:8-10).

"Brought life and immortality to light through the gospel!" Normally, we say something is "brought to light" when it is brought up out of concealment and set in clear view. A fact is brought to light in a court hearing. A situation is brought to light by a piece of news reporting. Well, the Scripture says that life has been brought to light. Through the gospel, through the good news, life has been brought up from where we had it buried. We had buried it beneath an overgrowth of things, beneath our preoccupation with small ideas and unworthy values. We had wrapped it in trifles, but he would clothe it with immortality. We had bludgeoned it down into the dark, but he would bring it up to the light.

You know that I could spend the rest of the day illustrating how, for many people, life is buried in the darkness. Permit me to cite just two or three such illustrations. You know that milleniums ago they buried the bodies of the ancient dead with their trinkets beside them; but in California a little while ago, at his request, they buried the body of a rich industrialist in a tuxedo with a monkey wrench in his hand. On another side of the problem, one said, "My life is without point or purpose, a dizzy whirl centered around nothing." And another: "My life is an enslaving chain of futility; and every new experience is another link added to the chain." Once I heard the inimitable Dr. George Buttrick say: "The man who runs from woman to woman and gets pie-eyed in the tavern is trying to reduce life to the animal level, and perhaps that's what sin is."

There came out recently a popular-type of song which might very well be a part of a present-day Rubaiyat. The theme: Is that all there is? The female singer describes a childhood experience in which she sees a house fire destroy a home. Then she sings, "I said to my father, Is that all there is to a fire?" She saw the circus, and having seen it, said, "Is that all there is to a circus?" Later, in adulthood, she came, presumably, into the experience of loving a man and being loved by him, and she said, "Is that all there is to love?" After each of the questions comes the refrain: "Is that all there is to that? Then let's keep dancing; break out the booze and let's have a ball." This is, of course, one way of dealing with disappointment, one way of reacting to reality. But not a good way. Is that all there is? No. There was more that she never saw. Yes, life can get terribly buried down in the murky deeps where it's dark.

But don't ever forget it: Christ has brought life up to the light through the gospel. Try to see your life in that light. If you can, you will see it whole, you will see all of it. For here in the gospel is a piece of good news which makes a mighty difference, powerful, dynamic.

Let me tell you a story, a very personal one, if I may. One year just before Easter I was burdened with work, weighed down with responsibility, beset with difficulty — or so I thought. I was bone weary and mentally tired. In this condition I went one day alone into a room to preview a motion picture film on the resurrecton of Jesus. Sitting there in the dark, I watched the familiar episodes of the drama unfold. But I was only half seeing, half hearing. Then there on the screen was the Apostle Thomas in prison telling his prison mates about it — Thomas, devoted follower of Christ, now facing death because he was. And suddenly, and so very unexpectedly, it came over me that all the problems which chafed and burdened me were swallowed up in a glorious victory. There I saw in the light of this vast, sweeping perception of life that no ordeal of circumstance can ultimately matter much. I walked out of that room that day with wings on my feet.

But you don't get his view of life unless you see it in the big, bright light. Some things you never find out if you always take a worm's-eye view of what you are. It takes a different view to know that "though our outer nature is wasting away, our inner nature is being renewed day by day" and that "these momentary afflictions are working for us an eternal weight of glory beyond all comparison" (2 Corinthians 4:16-17). Sometimes we are so involved with our problems that we don't see enough of life even to be thankful for being alive. Imagine the shock of one man who said to his friend, "That's an awful cough you've got," when his friend answered, "Maybe so, but down at the morgue this morning I saw half a dozen fellows who'd like to have it!" When you can see life in the full dimension of all it is, then, no matter what the problems are, you're glad you're alive. And the best way I know to see life full-size is to see it in the light of the gospel of Christ, in the light of his coming and presence.

This brings us, I think, to the second thing I would like to say. It is this: Not only should we see our life in his light, but we should also live our life in the light in which we see it. Life is to be lived. There are things to do, places to go. There is a journey to be made. There are steps to be taken. Concerning the coming of Christ into the world, John said that "the light was shining into the darkness" and "the true light which enlightens . . . was coming." Then thirty years after his coming, Jesus himself was saying, "I am the light of the world" (John 3:12). He was speaking of the same world John was — the world within, not some nebulous, vague something-or-other out yonder somewhere, but the real world of the inner us. He knew that in the final sense every man's walk is made within, and every choice is an inward choice. So our Lord puts his light where it belongs. To borrow from the language of our space age, he would illuminate our guidance mechanism.

Jesus says, "He who follows me shall not walk in darkness, but shall have the light of life" (John 3:12). He says, "You have the light; believe in it" (John 12:36). He knows we need it. We don't have enough light of our own. The Old Testament prophet also knew this and said it this way: "You who kindle a fire and encircle yourselves with sparks, and walk in the light of your own fire and of the sparks which you have kindled, you shall lie down in sorrow" (Isaiah 50:11). As we make the journey of a lifetime, we need a light beyond what we ourselves can generate. And the gospel is saying that in Christ we have that light — available within us. I have already tried to say that, seeing ourselves in this light, we can discover what we are, can see our life wholly, as what it is. Let me now go on to say that we may — and should — do our living of life in harmony with what, in his light, we have discovered our life to be.

Living with due regard to what we are — this is what we should be doing. Apparently people who live like animals have not yet discovered their own humanity. They grab and grasp and claw like animals. They take food like animals — with never a word of thanks. They take sex like animals — wherever it is available. They push and shove like animals — no matter who gets hurt. Their life expression is physical and biological as though there is nothing more. But there is something more; and we need to make this discovery.

A kid with pimples is playing about the neighborhood; but a new family moves in next door, and there is a lovely girl in the family, and this neighborhood kid suddenly discovers that he is a man. It would be too bad, wouldn't it, if he should go all the way to the end of his years and never make that discovery.

A man has long been preoccupied with his days at the office, his Saturdays on the golf course, his evenings puttering about his garage or his lawn, his Sunday morning sleep-ins, and his Sunday afternoons with the ball games — and then comes the message that his wife, whom he truly loves, but to whom he has never said much about his love, has been critically hurt in a terrible automobile crash, is lying unconscious in a hospital emergency room, and it is gravely uncertain whether her heart will beat again or she will take another breath. This man very abruptly discovers dimensions of his own being that he had never known were there. And it would be too bad, wouldn't it, if he should never make that discovery.

In the light of new circumstance, we can learn many things we never knew before. One may draw half a dozen straight lines on paper which, when seen, appear to be only a flat design having length and breadth. But a messenger comes and says, "Look again; look for something else." Then, as the viewer does this, all at once the flat thing becomes a cube, there is the dimension of depth, a dimension unseen before. The difference is made by the appearance of the messenger who says, "Look again."

Something of this kind our Lord Christ does for us. There was Matthew, collector of taxes, narrow, routine-minded opportunist, who never understood how big and broad life is until Jesus got to him; and then he did. There was Mary Magdalene, woman of the streets, beaten, broken, life narrowed down until it was almost at dead end, who never knew how rich and good life really is until she met Jesus; but then she did. There were those fishermen of Galilee, good fishermen, who knew how to row a boat, set a sail, tell about the weather, mend nets, and catch fish, who never quite understood that life is more than fishing until Jesus came and called them out from what they were into what they could become. And don't you see: Matthew and Mary and those fishermen all have one thing in common — after they met Jesus they began to live in new dimensions of their being.

In his letter to the Ephesians the Apostle Paul writes concerning the sort of context in which our life is cast and the kind of potential life has. His exulting words: "I pray God . . . according to the riches of his glory, that he will grant you to be strengthened with might by his Spirit in the inner man; that Christ may dwell in your hearts by faith; that you, being rooted and grounded in love, may be able to comprehend with all saints, what is the breadth, and length, and depth, and height, and to know the love of Christ which surpasses knowledge, that you might be filled with all the fullness of God" (3:14-18).

O how gloriously true, my friend — we live in vast dimensions of goodness and power, of meaning and love. We can range across broad spaces of thought and feeling.

But too much we make prisoners of ourselves, as though we had tethered ourselves to a stake somewhere with a very short rope. Would you like to be somebody special? Well, you are. Each of us is — somebody special to God. Read John 3:16 again: "God so loved the world that he gave his only begotten Son that whosoever believes in him should not perish, but have everlasting life." See yourself in the light of that; put yourself in that picture; think of yourself as a part of that world, the world he so loved. And I would say that that is being someone rather special. Then live in the light of this. I know of no better starting place for living than at what I shall call Realization-point One, the point where we realize who and what we really are.

There is yet another aspect of our living in the full brilliance of our Lord's illumination of our life. It is the important matter of our living in the light of God's availability. One thing that the coming of Christ is saying to us is that no human person of faith and good will need ever walk alone any more. He is "Immanuel" — God with us. The prophet Zephaniah said to the people of his time, "The Lord your God in the midst of you is mighty, and he will save you" (3:17). With the coming of our Savior he is in our midst as never before. Do you remember the Old Testament story of the three Hebrew men who were thrown by the irate king into the fiery furnace at Babylon? Next morning when the king looked in, he saw not only the three of them standing among the flames, but there with them he saw also "the form of the fourth" and he said that form was "like the Son of God" (Daniel 3:25). If I may for a moment employ that soul-stirring phrase, let me say that the "form of the fourth" may sometimes be but dimly seen in the fiery furances of our life, but he is there.

Sometimes we complain that God is not observed doing anything spectacular. Why, we say, Moses saw a burning bush — why don't we? Well, the answer may be because the bush we see is blooming instead of burning — and the blooming of a bush may very well be a greater wonder than the burning of one. But, someone says, God spoke to Moses from the bush that burned. Yes, I know; and I strongly suspect he is speaking to us from the ones that bloom. The very orderliness of God's universe is quite often mistaken for his absence. The Lord Christ, by his coming, is letting us know this: God has made himself available.

Live in the light of this. If you are doing the right things, there's nothing you have to do alone. If you are going the right places, he'll be in every step you take, and although you may falter, he will not. When you fall, he will be there to pick you up again. When you are weary, he will be strong. And when you must stop for sleeping, you can trust him to stay awake and to be there to take your hand again when the morning light calls you to go on.

Let me tell you now about a third aspect of our living in the light. We may — and should — live in the light of what we may *become*. Read again the prologue to John's Gospel: He who is the light is come; he is come unto his own; his own did not receive him — *but* (nevertheless, notwithstanding, in spite of this fact) all who receive him, who believe in his name, to them he gives *power to become* children of God.

Here is an exciting fact: we do not always have to be what we are. God gives the ability to become. This is a truth with many facets. Lincoln was a child of poverty, of a humble family, in the American backwoods, but he could become the stalwart statesman who saved the American union. George Frederick Handel was an unknown Prussian who seemed to have everything weighted against him, but he could become the skilled creator of the mightiest of all oratorios, *The Messiah*. Saul of Tarsus was an intemperate and bitter enemy of the Christian Faith, but he could become the most powerful champion of that Faith the world has yet known.

A second exciting fact is this: resident in the human breast is a built-in urge to become. As poet Harry Kemp writes, God "has put an upward reach into the heart of man." Sometimes people squelch the urge, brutally bludgeon it and beat it down. Sometimes they pervert it, distort it, and send it off in directions it was never meant to go. But God knows the urge is there. The story is told of a sculptor who worked many weeks on a block of marble, carving a bust of Lincoln. The delightful black lady who was employed to clean and care for his studio watched the process day after day as the head, shoulders, and facial features of Lincoln gradually emerged. Then, when the bust was almost finished, she said to the sculptor, "How come you knew Mr. Lincoln was in that block of marble?" Well, a sculptor knows nothing about marble that God doesn't know about us. He knows what's in there. He knows what we can become.

Michelangelo was walking with a friend along the street of an Italian city when they came upon a block of stone left by the workman from a construction project. The master of hammer and chisel paused, walked around the stone, looked at it carefully, touched it here and there, and said, "There is an angel in that stone, and I must bring it out." God knows about stones and angels, and he is forever working to bring the angels out. I repeat: He knows what we can become.

I suppose there are some things some of us cannot become, because of the limitations of our ability. I doubt if I could ever become a great musician or painter. In achievements such as these, each of us can become only his own best, his own most. Each can rise only to his own ceiling. But how high is this? Probably higher than most of us think. Each can range only to the end of his own tether. But how far is this? Probably much farther than most of us suppose. When Grandma Moses was seventy, it may have been assumed that her life was almost done. Not so. After that she became one of the most widely known landscape painters of her time. Winston Churchill was sixty-five and retired, and it may have been assumed that that was that. But it was after that when the indomitable Winnie answered the desperate call of his embattled country and became one of the most effective leaders England ever had.

Well, it is quite possible you may not become (although you may) another Winston Churchill or Grandma Moses, and maybe I will not become a Beethoven or a Michelangelo. But let me tell you something. Whatever your age, your limitations, your struggles, problems, health, background, or status, I point you to a wide open door, to a high-road that leads on, to summits with unlimited horizons; and I announce to you that the most wonderful privilege of power anyone may ever have is yours, that whatever else you may or may not become, this you can: *a child of God.* "As many as receive him, to them gives he power to become." And this includes you.

Some other person may begin life as a prince, born in a palace, having position and wealth, because he is a son of a king. You, although humbly born to poverty and problem, hindered by struggles, temptations and sins, can end your life as a prince (or princess) because you have become a child of The King. And there is no higher privilege or honor or position than this. Others may strive to become this or that; but you, receiving Christ, are given the power to become the best that any human person can ever be.

Some things must always be essentially what they are. The pebble by the roadside is just a stone; time and weather may change its shape a little, but it is still just a stone. But not so with you — this creature of divine design and plan; you can change. If God's man can fall as he did and does, he can also climb. If he could reach for the forbidden fruit in the Garden of Eden, he can also reach for the hand of God. If he can sin, he can also repent. If he can wander away as a prodigal, he can also come home. You can become! Here is life's most exciting fact. Never forget it; never lose it among the rubble of lesser things. Live in the light of this.

And know that you and I are incomplete until we have become what we are meant to be. We are created as creatures of God, and the creative work is not finished until we have become "new creatures in Christ Jesus." Our life remains unfulfilled while we have the capacity to become and are not becoming. Tragic and pathetic is the waste of powers not used, of resources untapped. Do you remember the story of the rich young ruler who came to Jesus seeking light for his way? Do you remember that, unwilling to turn loose and let go in response to the invitation of Christ, he went away sorrowfully? Phillips Brooks said of this young man: "His soul was like a tall, strong ship, but tied fast with a long rope. It was able to struggle up channel past headland and light and buoy that marked the way, but always something held it back from laying itself at rest beside the golden shore." Our life urges it upon us, that we live in the light of what we may become.

Some things you may become only for a little while; some achievements are so very temporary. Become physically strong, and time will wrest away your strength. Become materially rich, and death will take the riches all away. But become a child of God, and this you can be forever.

Pilgrim Living in a Vagabond World

Matthew 7:6-14 "Narrow is the way . . ."

I am thrilled to see a powerful airplane cut a straight path across the sky, above the mountains and the rivers, homing in on some distant destination. I am much moved when I watch a huge ocean liner disengage from the dock, slowly make its way out to the harbor's edge, and then swing about, point its stately prow toward an oceanside city three thousand miles away, and open all engines to full power. And I am inspired when I see a man who moves through life as though he is going somewhere and knows where he is going.

I want to talk with you now about pilgrim living in a vagabond world. I would base this upon something Jesus said in the Sermon on the Mount: "Enter in by the narrow gate, for the gate is wide, and the way is broad that leads to destruction, and there are many who travel by it. But straight is the gate and narrow is the way that leads to life, and those who find it are few" (Matthew 7:13-14). Here Jesus is talking the language of travel. He speaks of two roads and of the different places they lead. He is not issuing a new law by which life is to be governed; he is simply pointing to two roads that are already there, and advising us which we should choose as we make the journey of life.

Thomas Carlisle said, "Life is a little gleam of light between two eternities; out of an eternity we come and into an eternity we go." Carlisle may be right; but I would like to add: we have to get through this world first. Having made our entrance, we must find our way properly and rightly to our exit; and I want to talk about this.

Using Carlisle's figure of speech, in the beginning a door opens and we step out of eternity into time. Then the years pass — and another door opens and we bow out, and our traveling companions wave goodbye to us and we to them. Thinking of this, Emerson wrote a poem containing this line: "Goodbye, proud world, I am going home." A somewhat amusing song of the "country" variety puts it this way: "No matter how I struggle and strive, I'll never get out of this world alive!"

The process of moving from the opening of the first door to the opening of the last one is what we call *living*. All the way, we are going somewhere; we are on pilgrimage; and we ought to have a pilgrim's sense of purpose. Without a sense of pilgrimage we are lost — like a rudderless and motorless derelict drifting at sea. We are lost, I mean, in the conduct of life, in our moral directions and spiritual relationships.

There is a difference between a pilgrim and a vagabond. The pilgrim knows where he is going — or where he wants to go — and he is forever trying. The vagabond is a wanderer; his directions are determined by convenience; he does what is easiest or most expedient or appealing at the time. Someone once asked one of the old-time highway tramps how he decided which way to go when he came to a fork in the road. His answer: "I simply put my back to the wind." That will make a tramp out of anybody.

One summer day I became aware of a loud clattering sound coming through the open window of the dormitory room where I was spending a few days. Looking from the window to see the source of the clatter, I soon saw it. There, three flights down, on the ground, a hundred yards from the building, was a boy of about eight-year size kicking a tin can. Fascinated, I watched him. He would kick the can; then whichever way it went he would follow and kick it again; wherever it landed he would go. I watched the boy across a street and a couple of alleys, across a couple of lawns and a vacant lot — indifferently and somewhat absently following that can, and kicking it, following it, and kicking it again, and again. And I thought of life and how much like this boy a lot of people are. They aimlessly blunder into any given moment of experience, smash through it at its weakest point, and then go on in whatever direction seems easiest or most attractive.

A pilgrim, however, is a traveler — going from somewhere to somewhere. You remember Abraham? He had been a wanderer, a nomad of the Mesopotamian Valley; but God called him, and he became a pilgrim. He heard a call and obeyed it; and this is what makes pilgrims of people.

How about a little history lesson? In England there were people called Puritans. They wandered about the country, and then sought refuge in Holland. They spent a long time trying to do what was easiest for them. But then they made a decision: they would come to the wilderness of North America and build a new home for religious freedom in the world. They left Holland, made their way back to England, and there one hundred and two of them boarded a little ship called the Mayflower. And these homeless wanderers pointed that little vessel toward a new home across the sea. William Bradford, for thirty years the governor of their colony at Plymouth, wrote in his *History of Plymouth Plantation* concerning their leave-taking for America, and these are his words: "They knew they were Pilgrims." No longer were those people wanderers or refugees; they were pilgrims. Now they moved with purpose. They had heard the call of freedom, and they had resolved to pursue it to the very death — and they did.

John Henry Jowett, eminent British-born clergyman of a couple of generations ago, told of an experience which was his one dark night far out in the English countryside. Having been entertained in a rural home, as he was taking his leave, the farmer handed him a lighted lantern and said, "The lantern will help to keep you out of the ditch. The glimmer you see yonder in the distance is the light of Saddleworth Station. Make for that." I would make this point: a pilgrim is one who sees a glimmer in the distance and makes for it. Every footstep brings him closer to it. He may or may not reach his goal, but he is one who is on his way. The Apostle Paul had a magnificent sense of pilgrimage, and he expressed it this way: "Leaving what lies behind, and straining forward to what lies ahead, I press on toward the goal for the prize of the upward call of God in Christ Jesus" (Philippians 3:13-14).

Much of our world, however, is pretty much the vagabond kind. This is not a new development on the human scene. In his day the Apostle Peter found it necessary to say to the people to whom he ministered, "Save yourselves from this untoward generation" (Acts 2:40). In other words, cut yourself loose from these who aren't really going toward anything. Get your eye on a goal and make for it. Get some purpose and discipline into your walk. Some people don't have any, and many don't have much.

I listened to a radio program in which a modern young woman was being interviewed. The interviewer asked, "Are you married?" And she answered, "Sometimes." Her answer was quickly and glibly given, with no evidence that she saw anything unusual about it. She meant it: she was sometimes married, sometimes not married, as suited her convenience or her whim at the time. I'm sure you know about the philosophy of pragmatism, the philosophy of living which says: if it works it's okay. One of the most tragic troubles of the pragmatist is that he is myopic, nearsighted. He isn't looking far enough ahead. He doesn't have a long-range view. He isn't really going anywhere. He is just kicking a can. He is determining his values and taking his directions from the illumination of the moments rather than the milleniums.

If I entrust my life to the captain of an ocean-going ship to get me safely across the sea, I want him to steer by a star, and not by the contour of the next waves. If you fly in a great airliner to a distant place, you want your pilot to be tuned in on the homing beam; you don't want him to fly by the signs he sees in the clouds and the winds. But this is the way much of the world moves in the moral and spiritual and intellectual sense.

And, my friend, pilgrim living does not always come easy in a vagabond world. Our temptation is to accommodate to what is around us. In German the word *zeitgeist* means the spirit of the age, of the time. Our temptation is to take our traveling signals from the zeitgeist, to live by the spirit of the age rather than by timeless values. If our compass is to guide us well, its needle should be pointed to the distant pole; but too often it is deflected by local magnets.

Have you ever heard anyone say of another that he is a chameleon? The chameleon is that lizard which takes the color of whatever is around him; he has no integrity of his own. And this is a perilous business. Carl Sandburg wrote of the chameleon which came upon a scotch plaid and died in the crossroads. If you are going anywhere worthwhile, you cannot be a chameleon person. You must not be so weak as to permit whatever is nearest at the moment to set the moral tone of your life. The Apostle Paul wrote about this: "Do not be conformed to this world" (Romans 12:2). As J. B. Phillips translates it, "Do not let the world squeeze you into its own mold."

There is no way of living that is half as thrilling or adventurous as pilgrim living in a vagabond world — to hear the beat of a different drummer, to see the glimmer in the distance, to hear a call from afar, or, as Emerson put it, to "hitch your wagon to a star." There is no better quest than the one Paul spoke of when he said, "Seek what is above" (Colossians 3:1).

Although we may never reach all the summits we aspire to, the pilgrimage has rewards of its own. In a drama the question is asked, "Have you reached the heights?" And the answer given is this: "No, but I saw them once, and they are there all right." In a churchyard in Switzerland one may read this epitaph on a gravestone: "He died climbing." That's a good way to die; there is none better. In the United Methodist Church, when a prospective minister is being examined for ordination, this is one of the questions asked: "Are you going on to perfection?" One young man objected to this question as suggesting an impossible goal. But the wise old bishop said to him, "If you are not going on to perfection, then, pray tell me, what are you going on to?" Even if we never reach all the spiritual and moral summits we seek, we are surely not worse off for having tried; and every lesser summit we attain is at least that much higher than we would have been had we never begun the pilgrimage in the first place.

Yes, my dear friend, there is no higher thrill nor richer reward than to live as a pilgrim in a vagabond world.

But if we are going to be pilgrims we must get up and get going. I find it highly inspiring to go back about thirty-five hundred years and look in upon a piece of ancient history. It is recorded in Exodus, chapter fourteen. The Hebrew people had spent about four hundred years of slavery in Egypt. Now, under the leadership of Moses, they were on their way to the Promised Land which lay somewhere ahead of them. They had come to the Red Sea, and there they had camped. Before them was the apparently impassable water, behind them the pursuing army of the angry Egyptian king, and within them a seething restlessness and resistance, a hopelessness and despair. Moses went to God in prayer. And God said to him, "Why are you crying to me? Speak to the people that they go forward." You know the story; you know that Moses did speak to them, that the water somehow parted, and that they did go forward.

Here was a time when God told a man to stop praying — and start acting. God turned Moses around and said, "Speak to the people." Tell them it is time to stop wailing and start walking! There is no record that Moses argued about it, or that he said, "But, Lord, look at all that water!" Forthwith he got up and spoke, and the people got up and went, and somehow the water rolled back and let them pass. O yes, it's commendable to want something good to happen, to wish it will, and even to pray that it will, but the time comes when we must start acting as though it will happen.

Then, of course, later in the pilgrimage of those people toward the land of promise, they came to the Jordan River. They got out of Egypt by marching into the "impassable" sea and crossing it. Forty years later they got into Canaan in a similar way, as Joshua led them across the Jordan. There is a lesson in living here, and it is this: No river is going to let you cross it until you attempt the crossing. The time comes when you must break camp and start moving. Whatever the time, whatever the place, whatever the circumstance, and whatever other word God may have to say, there is one word which is always appropriate: "Speak to the people that they go forward." Forward in depths of commitment and venture of service, forward in directions from which God and life are calling and saying, come on.

And the word is go forward — not just look that way, and wish, and want — but get up and go. When we do, we may be surprised how the water will open and how much easier is the crossing than we thought it would be. Someone has said that a mountain never looks as high from anywhere as it does from the bottom. I'm saying: Act on the good things you wish for. John Wesley gave us some good advice on Christian living when he said: If you do not have faith, act as though you do until it comes, and it will.

Let me illustrate. Here is a church with half its pews empty on Sunday morning, and all the people say they wish the attendance were better and they wonder why it isn't. Well, if everybody who has sometimes said, "I wish we had better attendance," and "Why don't we?" would all come just once at one time, the pews would be more than filled, and everybody would be thrilled. And having done it once, they might realize they could do it again, and, doing it, they would be thrilled again, and the whole community would soon take note, and others would also come. I'm saying to you that good things happen when good people stop wailing and start walking.

For instance, if each citizen who sometimes bemoans the moral conditions of our time really got down to the business of practicing public and private morality in all areas of life, instead of exempting areas they make exceptions of, the social climate of this nation would be transformed in six months. Let me repeat it: Good things happen when good people stop wailing and start walking.

Permit me to tell you another story — and you can read this in your Bible in the seventh chapter of 1 Kings. It was about 900 B.C., and the city of Samaria was surrounded by the Syrian armies. The siege having gone on for a long time, there was famine inside the city walls, with people even eating their own children, while outside in the surrounding hills, the Syrians kept watch. Near the gate of Samaria sat four men who were lepers, and they were as hungry as anyone else. One day one of them said to the others, "Why do we sit here until we die?" And he proposed that they go out and cast themselves upon the mercy of the Syrians, reasoning, "If they save us, it will be well; if they kill us, we shall but die." So the four men arose in the morning twilight and made their way into the hills to the Syrian battle line. They found it deserted; the camps were empty; to the last man the enemy had fled. As it was later learned, the Syrians had heard strange sounds in the night, and believing that a huge army was approaching them, they fled across the Jordan, leaving their tents and supplies and much of their livestock and battle equipment.

The point I want to make is that it was only when four leprous men decided to do something, and so moved, got up and went, that the amazing discovery was made that the enemy wasn't there any more. Had four men not ventured forth, the whole population of Samaria would probably have starved to death, believing the enemy was still out there. How often, rather than get up and walk, we sit still and wail, for fear of enemies who may have long ago fled their camp.

I read a story about a proud, mighty Rocky Mountain eagle that was captured and tethered to a stake. The great bird was there many weeks. Then the man who held the eagle captive, sympathizing with the wild creature, decided to set it free. He cut loose the tether rope. The great bird stood there. About three days and nights went by before that majestic creature realized that he was free to fly. He stood around as though he were still tethered. As I read that story I thought: If I were a Rocky Mountain eagle, no matter what the circumstances or what I was tethered to, I would occasionally try my wings. About that time God began to talk with me, and he said, "Look, fellow, as a human being, you are far more than a Rocky Mountain eagle could ever be; *try the wings you've got.*"

No, my friend, whatever sea confronts us, we don't need a Moses to stand by and command us to go forward. God is doing that — already, and all the time. I don't care where we are or what time it is, how old or how young, or rich or poor, or what the conditions are, the word is go forward — and there is always somewhere forward to go. I suppose you know by now that I am talking about faith, about moving forward as though the way will open — for this is what faith is. I think it's time to read something our New Testament is saying to us about living: "Christ has opened a new and living way for us, taking out of the way whatever was against us, nailing it to his cross" (Hebrews 10:20; Colossians 2:14). You can move on that; believe me, my friend, you can move on that.

Yes, if we are going to be pilgrim people in this vagabond world, we must get up and get going. But there is also something else we must do. We must find a star to steer by. We need guidance for the way. Some time ago, after one of our American space vehicles was launched, it was discovered that its elaborate guidance system had locked in on the wrong star. Heaven only knows where that thing would have gone had a correction been impossible. But, fortunately, the correction was possible, and from down here on earth the proper adjustments were made, the vehicle got a fix on the right star, and the mission was successful.

In our time there is a lot of confusion concerning directions. Many of us are very much on the go, but where? I am reminded of the man who employed the owner of a small airplane to fly him to a business appointment a few hundred miles away. After they had been in the air for a time much longer than necessary to make the whole tirp, the man said to the pilot, "Where are we?" And the pilot replied, "Well, I think we are lost; but we're making good time." It doesn't count for much when you are making good time in the wrong direction. I think of the man who went into Northern Minnesota on a hunting trip and hired a local guide. After the two men became very lost somewhere in the woods, the hunter said to his guide, "You numbskull, I thought you said you were the best guide in Minnesota." To which the guide responded, "I am, undoubtedly; but I think we're in Canada now." No matter how good your guide may be for elsewhere, he's no good for you unless he's good for you where you are.

In our world we have a babel of confusion about directions. Loud voices in one breath are heard speaking of a "new morality" and something called the "nego." Shrill loudspeakers assert the "rights of man" and proclaim the "death of God." Powerful currents sweep across the human scene; subtle influences shape us, manage our spirits and mold our minds; and we scarcely know what winds are blowing or where they come from, and certainly we don't know where they are going. More and more the individual person is the product of univer-

sal man, and the black and white issues of moral caliber
and quality are tending to disappear into a dreary shade
of leaden gray.

There is a story about a schoolboy who asked his
teacher, "Is it wrong to cheat?" The teacher, wishing to
be modern and non-authoritarian, replied, "If you can
cheat and live with yourself, I suppose, that's all right."
The boy didn't cheat, and neither did he do very well; the
grade card he took home wasn't exactly of the *summa
cum laude* quality. Upon returning to school, he
approached his teacher again, saying, "I think hereafter
it will be easier to cheat and live with myself than not to
cheat and try to live with my grandmother." That boy
had a problem; he needed help; he was lost in the
shadowland of a serious dilemma, and he needed a light
to find his way out.

The fact is that somewhere between our vast systems
and our little devices many of us are quite lost, and we
need a fix on a guiding star. John Masefield gave us that
beautiful poem *Sea Fever*, the first two lines of which go
this way:

> I must go down to the seas again, to the lonely sea
>   and the sky,
> And all I ask is a tall ship and a star to steer her
>   by . . .

A voyaging vessel needs a relationship with the
universe, a fix on a dependable star. Without this a ship
can become lost in its own patch of sea. It needs
something beyond, something beyond itself. It cannot
safely sail by the flag that flies from its mast or the
searchlight which shines from its deck. It requires a firm
point of reference that will keep it in right relationship
with everything else from the most distant shore to the
nearest ocean island.

This is not only a requirement for ships sailing the
seas; it is also a requirement for us on our pilgrimage of
living. The Apostle Paul wrote of this in his second letter
to the church at Corinth. Those bickering and warring

Corinthians needed a guidance from beyond themselves. And Paul wrote to them that we Christians "must not compare ourselves with some who commend themselves; for, in measuring themselves by themselves, and comparing themselves among themselves, they are being very foolish" (10:12). Paul was pleading for some standard from beyond, beyond self and self-will, and certainly from beyond the immediate social scene. He was urging the Corinthians to look beyond themselves and those around them, to look to Christ and to see themselves in the light of him.

There are many differences between a club and a church, but the major difference is this: in a club each member is related to every other in fellowship and activity, but in a church each member is related to Christ, and all are therefore bound together with one another in fellowship and activity. In a club each member may very well measure himself alongside every other, but in a church there is another point of primary reference. Through the Old Testmant prophet Amos, God announced, "I will set a plumbline in the midst of my people" (Amos 7:8). Do you know what a plumbline is? It is judgment, it is *kriterion*. In the construction industry a plumbline is suspended alongside any verticle object to determine if it is exactly perpendicular. By a plumbline the uprightness of a thing may be judged. Without something plumb somewhere around, all things can be leaning and out of kilter and you scarcely know it.

Once I visited a kind of "fun house" in which nothing was level and nothing was straight up and down. Everything tilted or leaned — floors, walls, windows, doors. All things there were in proper alignment with one another, but nothing was in alignment with the world outside. Because everything inside the house sloped or leaned to exactly the same degree, everything appeared completely normal. And — you know the effect — as I stood in the middle of the floor, I felt that it was I who was leaning! Very quickly I was dizzy. Running water appeared to be flowing uphill. A ball would not lie at all on a surface which appeared to be perfectly level, but rolled away into a corner as though pushed by an unseen hand. When I tied my penknife to the end of a string and held it up before me, it appeared to hang there at a rakish angle, as though the law of gravitation had gone all out of whack.

There was, of course, nothing wrong with the law of gravitation. But there was something wrong with the house and everything in it. And the very disconcerting illusion was created by the fact that nowhere in view was there anything plumb or anything level. What I am trying to say is that you need a standard by which you can properly relate to reality. Without a point of reference you don't know where you are. Without a guiding star you can easily become very, very lost.

On the easel of a landscape artist was an array of precious stones — ruby, sapphire, emerald. Someone asked the artist why those stones were always there, and he answered, "These are my color reference, lest my memory fail, my eye lose its sense of tone, and my colors fade." Why do musicians use pitch pipes and tuning forks? You know — lest there be deviation from true pitch. For if the maker of music doesn't get started on the right tone level, he can easily run off somewhere into the wild blue yonder long before he reaches the end of his number. I am told that in the National Bureau of Standards in Washington, D.C., there is a golden yard-stick. Why? Because it is necessary that there be somewhere a final arbiter as to what a yard really is. The official yard is not determined by a comparison among merchants. The length of the yard in course of time could do strange things if this were the way it were done. But the yard of each merchant must be measured by one which is beyond them all.

The point is that we must live with an eye upon the ultimate, the eternal, upon a dependable star — or else we can deviate our way into ruin. Are you familiar with

that parlor game called pinning the tail on the donkey?
On a wall is a large picture of the animal, without tail.
The players are lined up at an opposite wall, and each in
turn is blindfolded, handed a "tail" and told to go and pin
it in the right place. Much to the amusement of other
players, any player may wander all over the room and at
last pin the tail almost anywhere, including the donkey's
head or rib cage or even somewhere on another wall. If
the player starts out wrongly or walks unsurely, he can
be greatly surprised when the blindfold is taken off and
he sees where he is.

Navigational errors are cumulative; when you are
wrong, the farther you go the more off course you get.
Several of a shepherd's flock of sheep had wandered
away and gotten lost, and someone asked the shepherd,
"What makes them do that?" The shepherd answered,
"They just nibble themselves lost." And so do people. A
little here, a little there; a tuft of this and a sprig of that,
and before he knows it, the nibbler is lost. And like the
poor, lost sheep, he lifts up his head from his nibbling,
looks around upon the rough and rocky scene, and knows
neither where he is nor how he got there. You see,
nobody ever really plans to make a tragic smash of life; it
just happens while people nibble, not really going
anywhere, and seeing no farther than the next sweet
morsel to be nibbled at.

I know that the prospect of walking in the "narrow
way" comes through to many people as boring and
unexciting. Many have the notion that what is right is
dreary and unadventurous. I recall hearing of an elderly
lady who had never eaten ice cream. When the opportunity came to partake of it, she took one taste, pushed
the dish away, and said, "Anything that good can't be
right!" Yes, it can, of course it can. The good can be
pleasing, exciting, adventurous. People who think that
all excitement is at the bar and none at the altar do not
know what life is.

But there is ample evidence that there are a great many such people. There is a very good book entitled *Immortal Wife*, a biography of Mrs. John C. Fremont. Having misread the title, a woman entered a bookstore and asked for a copy of *"immoral* wife." Learning that the word was *immortal* rather than *immoral,* she lost all interest in making the purchase. To her immorality was exciting to read about, but not immortality.

Everyone knows about the three monkeys — See No Evil, Hear No Evil, Speak No Evil. Now, somewhat recently, the trio has become a quartet. A fourth monkey has been added. His name: Have No Fun. In novelty stores you can buy little statuettes of the four monkeys — one with his hands over his eyes, one with his hands covering his ears, one with his hands tightly clapped over his mouth, and the fourth just looking gloomy and sour and mad. And the notion is that if you don't see or hear or speak some evil, you just don't have any fun.

But this notion is as far from the truth as any notion can ever be. The happiest people I have ever known are the people who are steering by the highest stars. And I predict they'll be happy a lot longer than all the others. No way of living is more adventurous or exciting than to choose the highest road and follow it.

I am trying to say that if we are going to be pilgrims in a vagabond world, we need a star to steer by. Some may say that we already have it, that it is built into us, that it is simply our conscience. Don't be too sure about that. As a guide, conscience is usually better than nothing, but sometimes not much better. Conscience is not a constant; it is a variable. It can be sensitized or deadened. It can be trained to say what we want it to, assuming somewhat the same role as the dummy that sits on the knee of a ventriloquist. Not many people violate conscience very much; they simply tone it down, shoot it with novocaine, recondition it, and make it parrot what they want it to say. A first lie may trouble the liar a bit; but after ten thousand lies, conscience doesn't have much to say on that subject anymore. Actually, there is very little remorse among criminals. As the Apostle Paul put it, conscience may be "seared as with a hot iron" (1 Timothy 4:2).

A conscience that is seared and insensitive is not a very dependable guide when one is trying to make his way through the moral jungle of our time or any time. Each of us has a high degree of responsibility to his own conscience — to keep it informed, sensitive, well-tuned, and alive — that it may serve us well. We have a responsibility not to abuse conscience by working it so hard that it becomes weak and weary and impotent from the discouragement of having spoken on one subject so many times and having been ignored so much.

But no matter how well we preserve the integrity of conscience, it remains essentially only a guard against wrong. We still need an incentive for right, an inspiration for going forward, for choosing the highest. Essentially conscience has a one-word vocabulary, and that word is "No." But the mere rejection of wrong does not make pilgrims out of people; it is the mighty appeal of the right that does this. Keep your conscience as sharp as you can — it will help to keep you from falling into the ditch. But you still need a gleam in the distance, a star to steer by.

Some may say that the guiding star is community, the corporate expression of human awareness, the common conscience of society. Don't count on it. What is it that community says? I can put the answer in two words: be average. Fall too far below the average, and community will put you in jail. Rise too high above the average, and community will look at you askance and somewhat in awe, and it will scratch its collective head and wonder what in the world to do about you. Community is saying: Line up; fit in; go along; conform.

In seeking a star to steer by, is this the best we can find? I think not. The Christian Faith offers something infinitely better. Paul spoke of it as "the upward call of

God in Christ." Listen; lift up your eyes and look. Catch the far vision. Set your eye upon a summit and your feet upon the trail that goes that way. And if you would be a pilgrim in a vagabond world, be ready to meet the storm and see it through. Someone has said, "If you would be a Viking, dare to face the north wind." But understand this: as you face it, you can know that the Master of all winds is with you, the Lord of the pilgrims is already on the trail.

Name Above Every Name

Luke 2:21
"He was called Jesus . . ."

The first thing about anyone is his name. A human person is born into the world, and almost immediately a word is chosen to denote him. Not a number, not a sign, not a shape — but a word. And that word becomes everyone's way of saying who he is. For all of his lifetime that word is used to indicate him. By means of it, he says, "This is I." By means of it, others say, "That is he." In a very real sense the word equals the person, stands for him as his equivalent. This is so very true that I can say, "I am Leonard Mann." Who am I? What am I? This I am: Leonard Mann.

The word assigned to denote an individual person is always the only total representation of him. When you say that a certain fellow is six feet tall — or three feet wide — you have made a representation in regard to his size. But it is only by using the denoting word that you represent him. It is only by using the denoting word that he totally represents himself. If he is obligating himself to pay off a forty thousand dollar mortgage on his house, at the bottom of a long finely printed sheet of paper he writes the denoting word, his name, and only that word will do. If he is getting married, he says, "I the denoting word, take thee, the denoting word, to be my wedded wife." If he is being awarded a college degree — or is being sentenced to hang — the decree is issued to the denoting word. And the word means the person.

It is utterly fascinating that in the Gospel According to John it is written: "In the beginning was the WORD, and the WORD was with God, and the WORD was God . . . and the WORD became *flesh* and dwelt among us" (John 1:1,14). It seems to me that in a very singular manner it is being said the He was beforehand. The

Johannine choice of "logos" reflects one of the most profound philosophical insights to be found anywhere in all literature. It is not merely incidental, I think, that John says that it was the word which became flesh. He might have chosen to say it was the number or the sign or the shape or something else that became flesh, but he didn't. And I think he didn't because it was in fact the word, and he selected "logos" because it was the only language that would fit the fact. Normally, a man is born and then the denoting word is added; in the instance of Jesus, however, it would appear the word was first and the flesh was added.

When a word is spoken it is one's utterance of himself; it is expression. It is therefore quite correct to say that, in giving his Son, the heavenly Father was expressing himself. But don't overlook this fact: you cannot express what isn't. For anything to be expressed, it must be. It cannot come forth unless it is. And Logos was, so John says; and Logos came among us, becoming flesh.

He entered our world at the same gate all babies do, the gate of birth. When they held him up and spanked him, I suppose he cried as all babies cry. But who was he, this newborn child? Those Bethlehem shepherds had some feelings about that; they went around calling him a Savior. Those wise men from the East had some opinions about it; they went to a lot of trouble to hail him and greet him as a newborn King. His mother had some private feelings about him which she "kept and pondered in her heart." Joseph had his feelings too, for, after all, in a dream he had listened to an angel visitant tell him even what name should be given to the Child. For it was required that even the incarnate Logos must have assigned to him a denoting word.

After eight days they took him to the place of circumcision, and they said to those attending there, "This is Jesus." And the authorities responded, "So he is." And he was. Upon entering the world, each of us is given a name; and it is up to us to give that name a meaning by the way we live and how we bear it across our span of years. This Bethlehem Child was called by a very common word; there was a boy named Jesus in almost every city block. But this Child took that word, and in about thirty-three years gave it a meaning that nobody had ever given it before and that nobody ever has since. The word "Jesus" means Savior. Savior he was, and for this reason this word was assigned to him as his name. Nobody ever fulfilled the meaning of a name any more completely than Jesus fulfilled that one.

Alexander means "helper of men;" but not every man who has borne that name has in fact been notable for his helpfulness to others. Katherine means "pure;" but not every woman named Katherine has been exactly pristine in her purity. Many boy babies have been named Jesus, but not many have distinguished themselves as saviors. One may have rescued a lamb which had fallen among the rocks; another may have picked up and taken to an inn a wounded man whom he found lying by the road. In some small ways some may have performed saving roles of one kind or another. But only this Bethlehem Child has ever so fulfilled the meaning of this name that it could be said of it, as Peter said to the elders and rulers of Jerusalem, "There is no other name under heaven given among men whereby we must be saved" (Acts 4:12).

The Bethlehem Child took that common word and wrought a kind of miracle upon it. Before the Child's birth, Joseph had heard a heavenly messenger give this instruction: "Call his name *Jesus*, for he shall save his people from their sins" (Matthew 1:21). And he did, and he has, and he does. A kind-hearted shepherd named Jesus may save a lamb from among the rocks; but this Jesus saves his people. A kind-hearted traveler named Jesus may save an unfortunate victim of robbers from the roadside ditch; but this Jesus saved his people from their sins. Jesus *is* Savior.

The Person has made that name-word something special, a name above every name. It is common in the Western world that parents choose "Bible names" for their children — John, Mary, Joseph, Paul. These names are everywhere in use. But may I suggest you look in your telephone directory — how many people named Jesus do you find listed there? Somehow this miracle word is set apart for special use, at least in much of the world. It is uttered in times of prayer and heard amid notes of highest praise; it is lisped by little children just learning to speak, and it is murmured with the last breath of people who are dying. And when people who are profane want to give expression to their profanity, and choose to do it with words, one of the words they use is Jesus. Profaneness may be expressed in many ways; and when the way is with words, the technique is to take the holy words that denote the Divine Being and treat them with utmost irreverence and disrespect. I've never heard any cussing done in the name of George Washington or Abraham Lincoln, but I've heard a lot of it that used the name Jesus. If the uses of the word, reverent or irreverent, are any clue to its special character, then this word is indeed a special one.

It is written in Luke 2:21 that eight days after the birth of the Bethlehem Child "when he was circumcised, he was called Jesus." This was the name given to him. Jesus was his "given" name. A surname is inherited; the child takes the surname of his parents. Of course, in that ancient time and land surnames were not used as we use them now. A man was simply known by his given name and further identified by the town he lived in. Thus we have Jesus of Nazareth. The word "Christ" is not actually a part of his name; it is a kind of title, meaning 'anointed" or "chosen" one. It is the Greek word *Christos*. This was not a part of his given name, but was given to him in common usage later, with the growing awareness that he was someone very special. So we put together his given name, the name of the town where he lived, and the title which came to be his, and we have this: Jesus Christ of Nazareth. To be completely correct, it should read: Jesus, *the* Christ. The definite article belongs there — both in the grammatical and the historical sense.

They started something, who on his circumcision day name this Child. They set in motion a sound wave which has never died away, although nearly twenty centuries have gone by. If you shout from a mountainside, other mountains may pick up the sound and echo it from hill to hill until at last it fades away in some distant ravine. But in so many ways the sounding of the name Jesus has been an ascending crescendo across the years. Sometimes the reverberating echoes of that name may have grown dim; but then they have swelled to greatness again; and there is an everlasting quality in this name which will never let it die.

As the Christ-man took the cross, an instrument of death, and turned it into the world's most powerful symbol of victory, so has he taken this common name-word and made of it the world's most cherished signal of hope and sign of spiritual and moral power. The Apostle Paul always rose to his highest summits of eloquence when speaking of Christ. In his letter to the Ephesians, Paul writes of "the immeasurable greatness" of the divine power which is at work within us, which was "accomplished in Christ" who has been exalted to a place "far above all rule and authority and power and dominion, and above every name, that at the name of Jesus every knee should bow" (2:9-10).

Name that is above every name! This was a very important fact for people like Peter and John and Paul. In that name there was power — and, of course, there still is. It was this name which they invoked when they called upon a power greater than themselves. At Philippi the Apostle Paul was pestered by a young woman "who had a spirit of divination and brought her owners much gain by soothsaying." Paul said to the spirit, "I charge you in the name of Jesus Christ to come out of her" (Acts

16:18). Peter and John were going up the temple steps at the hour of prayer when they came upon a lame man asking alms, and Peter said to him, "I have no silver and gold, but I give you what I have; in the name of Jesus Christ of Nazareth, walk" (Acts 3:6 R.S.V.). And the lame man walked.

As a result of this episode on the temple steps, the authorities at Jerusalem arrested Peter and John. Examining their prisoners, the key question the officers asked was this: "By what power or in what name did you do this?" Peter's answer rang like a bell: "Rulers of the people and elders, if we are being examined today concerning a good deed done to a cripple, by what means this man has been healed, be it known to you all, and to all the people of Israel, that by the name of Jesus Christ of Nazareth, whom you crucified, whom God raised from the dead, by him this man is standing before you well" (Acts 4:7-10 R.S.V.). Here, as on many other occasions, the apostolic testimony was that their mighty works were not theirs, but were wrought through the name of Jesus.

The authorities made quite an issue of this. They wanted to put an end to such mystifying and disturbing activity. They conferred with one another, saying, "What shall we do with these men? For that a notable sign has been performed through them is manifest to all the inhabitants of Jerusalem, and we cannot deny it. But in order that it spread no further among the people, let us warn them to speak no more to anyone in *this name.*" What did the authorities then do to the apostles? "They called them and charged them not to speak or teach at all *in the name of Jesus*" (Acts 4:15-18). Here is where they drew the line; it was the name which was the issue. Those judges didn't tell Peter and John to stay off the streets. They didn't tell them they couldn't teach or speak at all. But they did tell them not to do anything in the name of Jesus. It was this they feared; it was by this they were threatened. Those scheming and selfish authorities apparently did not feel threatened by those two fishermen from Galilee; it was the power of that name which worried them. So they said: stop using it.

But their warnings were wasted on Peter and John. Those men went right on just as though the authorities had never spoken, and soon they were again hailed before the council. The high priest said to them: "We strictly charged you not to teach in this name, yet you have filled Jerusalem with your teaching" (Acts 5:27 R.S.V.). This time they beat the apostles, they whipped them. And again "they charged them not to speak in the name of Jesus, and let them go" (Acts 5:40 R.S.V.). And go they did — everywhere — speaking of Jesus, and in the name of Jesus, to everyone who would listen and to many who would rather not have listened.

It is written that Peter and John, having been beaten and sternly admonished that day, "left the presence of the council, rejoicing that they were counted worthy to suffer dishonor for the name" (Acts 5:41 R.S.V.). Many apostles and disciples there were who felt this way about that name. They are described in Acts 15:26 K.J.V. as "men who hazarded their lives for the name of our Lord Jesus Christ." And Peter wrote this: "If you are reproached for the name of Christ, you are blessed" (1 Peter 4:14 R.S.V.). They carried the name of Jesus proudly and gladly — and so should we. A teacher in theological seminary used to say to us students: "Your job when you go out into the world is to take care of the good name of Jesus Christ." I think that during these post-student years I have recalled that statement at least ten thousand times.

The name was prized and precious in that ancient New Testament community of faith. As those people understood it, Christ bore a name more excellent than angels (Hebrews 1:4). Explaining why the Gospel of John was written, the writer says, "These things are written that you might believe that Jesus is the Chirst, the Son of God; and that believing you might have life through his name" (John 20:31 K.J.V. updated). Speaking to Cornelius at Caesarea, Peter declared that many bear witness to Christ, "that through his name whosoever believes in him shall receive forgiveness of sins" (Acts 10:43 K.J.V.). In the thought of those New Testament people, anything done in the name of Jesus had a special meaning. And Paul wrote to the Colossians: "Whatever you do, in word or deed, do everything in the name of the Lord Jesus" (3:17 R.S.V.).

Yes, the name was of unsurpassed importance among those first followers of the Way. Sometimes actors and performers argue among themselves as to whose name should be above another on the theater marquee; but in the minds of those first Christians there was no argument as to whose name belonged on top — of everything. "Name above every name," this was the name of Jesus. And it still is. Some have made that discovery; some have not. But whether or not the fact is known, fact it is: the name above every name is the name that was given to the Bethlehem Child, borne by him through Gethsemane to a cross, and beyond the cross to the golden glow of the next first-day morning, and from there through nearly two thousand years of earth-measured time.

Witnesses to the wonder and power of this name do not all speak from the dust of time long past. Current voices echo the sound first heard so long ago. Multiplied millions have sung with Charles Wesley:

Jesus the name that charms our fears,
That bids our sorrows cease,
'Tis music in the sinners' ears,
'Tis life, and health, and peace.

One of the greatest Christian hymns was written in Canterbury, England, by Edward Perronet in 1779. The first stanza:

All hail the power of Jesus' name!
Let angels prostrate fall;
Bring forth the royal diadem,

And crown him Lord of all.

Let me tell you a story which dramatically illustrates the power of this name. Half a century ago there wās in our country a singing evangelist named Luther B. Bridgers. His home was at the village of Wilmore, Kentucky. He was away from his home most of the time doing his evangelistic work wherever he was needed. Returning from one of his trips, Luther Bridgers discovered that the family home had been destroyed by fire. In that fire his wife and four children had died. In a Wilmore cemetery stands the unusual gravestone which marks the common burial place of those five most dear to him. But out of that tragic loss, and as a result of the faith that sustained him through it, Luther Bridgers wrote one of the best of our gospel songs: *He Keeps Me Singing.* The story is that he sat on the stone doorstep of what once had been his and his family's home, and there wrote both the words and music of this moving song:

There's within my heart a melody
Jesus whispers sweet and low,
Fear not, I am with thee, peace, be still,
In all of life's ebb and flow.
All my life was wrecked by sin and strife,
Discord filled my heart with pain;
Jesus swept across the broken strings
Stirred the slumbering chords again.
Though sometimes he leads through waters deep,
Trials fall across the way,
Though sometimes the path seems rough and
    steep,
See his footprints all the way.
Jesus, Jesus, Jesus — Sweetest name I know,
Fills my every longing, keeps me singing as I go.

One of our gospel hymns, sung to a tune called "Precious Name," begins with these lines:

Take the name of Jesus with you,
Child of sorrow and of woe;
It will joy and comfort give you;

Take it, then, where'er you go.

As I think of it now, I am quite sure that Peter and John
and Paul would have liked the message of this song.
Because this is just what they did — they took the name
of Jesus with them wherever they went. And you and I
may do this also, and we should. They considered
themselves honored to bear it, and so should we, and as
we bear it, care for it well.

We have said there is a magic, a wonder, a miracle
quality about this name. But how? why? what is it? Let
me try to answer this question with one illustration of
the unique significance and authority of the name. I
would speak with you of the singular role this name plays
in the mighty drama of prayer. You and I need God. We
need the touch of his hand upon our lives, his
forgiveness, his blessing, his help. We seek through
prayer, and through prayer receive. We are told in 1
Timothy 2:5 that there is "one mediator between God and
men, the man Christ Jesus." We are told in Hebrews 7:25
that "he is able for all time to save those who draw near
to God through him, since he always lives to make
intercession for them." We are told in 1 John 2:1 that
"we have an advocate with the Father, Jesus Christ, the
righteous." Mediator, Intercessor, Advocate — this
means that he fulfills the role of attorney pleading our
case before the throne of the heavenly King.

Some may argue that this is oversimplified drama.
Perhaps. But I do believe it is a good way to make a point
which needs to be made. And while we are about it, will
you permit me to press the drama somewhat further,
and make the point a bit more vivid? I know as well as
you do that we must not think of God as having a body or
the form of man. I know this is totally unacceptable
anthropomorphism. But only a moment ago I said that
"we need the touch of his hand upon our lives," and I
doubt if that terminology gave you any difficulty. We do
it all the time; we often use the metaphor of body when
we speak of the being and actions of God. It's simply an

aspect of the picture language we find it necessary to use when we attempt to communicate spiritual truth. And I'm convinced it's quite all right, so long as we understand that it is indeed metaphor which we are using.

So let me now use the metaphor to create a drama — to illustrate the intercessory role of Christ and the tremendous importance of his name to you and me as we approach our heavenly Father in prayer.

Very often we go to someone in the name of another. I may be unknown and uninfluential, and the president or the king of the Very Important Person, VIP, wouldn't have time for me or interest in me. I may knock at his door, and beg — but to no avail. But if I can come to him in the name of someone of importance he knows, if I can send in a note, or give some evidence of association with this important one, then the Very Important Person will let me in. He will agree to see me for the sake of the important person he knows and trusts, the one in whose name I have come. He will see me out of respect and regard for him; he will see me for his sake.

My dear friend, it is not without reason that when we go to our heavenly Father in prayer, we pray *in the name* of our Savior Jesus Christ. There is a reason why we ask what we ask *for Jesus' sake.*

Now let us come to the drama of which I spoke. I am a sinner; I am unworthy; I have failed. I have disappointed God over and over; I have ignored his known will; I have very ungratefully rejected many offerings of his great love. He has been patient with me, and I have presumed upon his patience. He has given me chance after chance, and, one after another, I have muffed my opportunities to do better. He has trusted me with freedom, and I have abused it over and over again.

And now I am in trouble. The voice of my conscience is speaking up from within me; some of my sins have overtaken me, their consequences apparent as never before. I am afraid of what may happen next, and for once in my life I realize that I need help.

So I approach God in prayer. I ask him to do things for me, to listen to me, to hear my cry. And up yonder somewhere, seated on his throne, God says, "Why should I?" And I know what he means. Is there any reason why he should? any reason why he should pay attention to me? I've been such a stinker! He has tried to help me in many ways many times, and I have paid no attention to him, and now I am expecting him to pay attention to me. I could have done many wonderful things for him in the world, but I haven't done them, and now I am asking him to do all sorts of wonderful things for me. And, really, I can't blame him if he says, "Why should I?"

But there is another Person in this drama. Jesus is sitting at the Father's right hand on the throne. And he hears me pray — in his name and for his sake. With his left elbow he gently nudges the Father, and says, "Father, you see that fellow down there praying?" And the Father replies, "Yes, I see him; what about it?" Then Jesus says to the Father, "Did you notice that he is praying in my name? You do remember me, don't you? You remember how you sent me down to that world, to people like that fellow — including him? You do remember how I loved those people, all of them, including him? You remember how my loving them got me into difficulty with various earthly powers, and how they nailed me to a cross and crucified me? Well, Father, maybe that fellow down there doesn't have any right to be coming to you and asking anything of you; but, Father, for my sake won't you please grant him the forgiveness he is asking in my name?"

And the Father says, "All right, Son, for your sake, I'll do it." And he does. A wave of peace sweeps over me, a warmth arises within me, and I know that my prayer is heard.

Simple drama maybe, too simple perhaps; but, O my dear friend, it is essential truth. Small wonder, then, that millions hail the power of Jesus' name and sing of the name that charms our fears and bids our sorrows cease. Name above every name, this one!

A good, kind, quiet woman had walked humbly but joyously with her Lord from her girlhood days. Now in her mid-nineties, strength failing, she lay upon the bed from which she would never be able to lift her body again. In early life she had committed to memory the words of Romans 3:2: "The law of the Spirit of life in Christ Jesus has made me free from the law of sin and death." For some reason, as the years had passed, this verse of Scripture had become more and more meaningful to her, and she was heard often reciting these words.

During her final days of waning strength, the precious old one continued to quote her favorite verse. As strength failed, she was able to utter the words only in a whisper: "The law of the Spirit of life in Christ Jesus has made me free from the law of sin and death." As strength continued to decline, words at the beginning and the ending were gradually dropped, and she was saying something like ". . . Spirit of life in Christ Jesus has made me free . . ." As the final hours approached, even this was shortened, until she was whispering, ". . . life in Christ Jesus . . ." And finally only one word was left; only one word did she have the memory or the strength to say: ". . . Jesus . . ." When all the other words were gone from her mind, this one lingered still. When she was too weary to open her eyes and look upon those about her, they who stood by listened to this one whispered word until there was no more breath with which to say it. But, you know, I'm sure that word was enough. For in that one word is a world of faith and trust and meaning. And for one who understands there always is.

Now let me add just one thing more. In our four Gospels Jesus is quoted as saying a good many things about himself. He identified himself in a good many ways: "I am the way . . . I am the truth . . . I am the life

. . . I am the good shepherd . . . I am the door . . . I am the bread of heaven . . . I am the water of life . . ." But there was one time when, I believe, Jesus identified himself in a very special way. It was when he, the risen Christ, victorious, glorified, met Saul of Tarsus on that Damascus Road and stopped him there. Out of the brilliance of the light that shone that noonday, he said, "Saul, Saul." Saul answered, "Who are you, Lord?" And very simply the Lord replied, *"I AM JESUS"* (Acts 9:4-5).

He gave no identification other than that name. He offered no qualification; he didn't have to; he never does, because he is Jesus. He stands in the naked power of his own Divine Manhood. And he stands ready to show you stars you never saw before.